the Story of Western Civilization

by Alan W. Riese and Herbert J. La Salle

Greece and Rome Build Great Civilizations

Book II

EDUCATORS PUBLISHING SERVICE
Cambridge and Toronto

Printed in USA

ISBN 978-0-8388-1496-3

10 11 12 PPG 12 11

Table of Contents

For the Student

Before you begin working in this book, you should know some things about it. You should know how the book is arranged and the best way to use it. Then your study of Greek and Roman civilization will be easier and you will learn more. Each chapter in this book has been planned to help you get the most from your reading. If you finish each section of each chapter in order and carefully, you will develop study habits that can aid you in becoming a better reader and a better student, not only in history class but in every class.

Each chapter begins with the title: GETTING READY FOR THE CHAPTER. This page has illustrations of things you will read about in the chapter ahead. It also has a few vocabulary words that are used in the chapter story. You need to know the meanings of these words if you want to understand the chapter. The directions say to find the words in your dictionary and write a good meaning for each. If you skip this important page, you will not be ready to begin reading the chapter story. It will have words in it that you may not understand.

After the picture/meanings page, each chapter has a story. You may read the story with your class or by yourself. Words you might have trouble with often will be followed by a guide to the way you say the word. This guide shows you how to say the word by spelling it a new way. For example:

civilization (siv-u-luh-ZAY-shun)

> The letters in CAPITALS show you which part of the word is said loudest.

After each chapter story are a few pages of exercises. These exercises have been carefully written to help you with your reading and your study of the chapter. The first exercise in every chapter has this title: *ANSWER THESE TO HELP WITH YOUR READING*. Good readers always look for the main ideas when they read. When you look for the answers to each question in this part of the chapter, you will be looking for the main ideas of the story. If you write your answers in complete sentences, you will be learning the most from the chapter.

The next parts of each chapter are introduced by the directions: *CIRCLE THE RIGHT WORD OR WORDS TO COMPLETE THE SENTENCES BELOW* and/or *CIRCLE TRUE OR FALSE*. You already know how to do these kinds of exercises. You need only draw a circle around the word or the letter to complete them. When you have found the right word or letter to circle, you will have picked out important details from the story.

Following these exercises, which help you find details from the story, is an important review of the vocabulary words. The directions read: *USE ONE OF THE VOCABULARY WORDS FROM THE BEGINNING OF THIS CHAPTER TO COMPLETE EACH OF THE SENTENCES BELOW.* If you have found and written a good meaning for each vocabulary word before you begin the chapter, this exercise will be easy. The sentences you are asked to complete will give a good meaning for each word as it is used in the story.

After you have finished the exercises, you will come to the last part of the chapter. It has this title: *THINK ABOUT AND DISCUSS IN CLASS.* This part of the chapter can be the most fun for you and your class. Most of the time it will show you how what you have read about history is important to you today in your daily life. Sometimes you will be asked to remember some things. Other times, you will need to look for some extra information in the library or in some other book. Always, you should feel free to discuss your ideas with your classmates and listen to what ideas they have. In this way, you can help each other to understand history even better.

When you and your classmates use this history reader the way it was written to be used, your study of civilization will be a good experience. You will learn where many things you use every day have come from. You will understand how governments came into being and how they help make life easier. You will know how long and how hard people have worked to make your life today as safe and secure as it is.

People March On!

March on their never-ending way,
Now with some millions of our ancestors,
Of Greece and Rome nearest, each going this way but once;

Each born a helpless baby, different from all other babies;
Each weaving his thread into the seamless cloth
Which we call civilization, making it stronger or weaker,
More beautiful or more ugly each day, just as you are doing.

Each was therefore special, of importance and necessary
To make the story what it is, and life
What it has become today.

If you had lived then, your chances of being born a slave
Would have been better than ten to one,
People still lived in a world of slavery with little personal wealth.

— adapted from a poem
by Edwin W. Pahlow

Adapted. From *Man's Great Adventure, Revised*, by Edwin W. Pahlow, © copyright 1938, by Edwin W. Pahlow. Used by permission of the publisher, Ginn and Company (Xerox Corporation).

King Minos built a large palace at Cnossus. It had many rooms, and the walls of the rooms were painted with colorful pictures and complicated designs.

The Minoans loved festivals. At some of these they watched acrobats do tricks on the backs of bulls.

The Minoans were known for the beautiful textiles they wove. These were used to make richly decorated clothing.

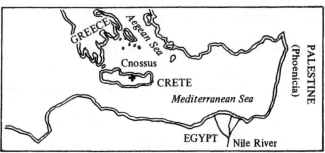

Many early civilizations developed along the edges of the Mediterranean Sea.

Getting Ready For Chapter One

1

Here are four vocabulary words that are used in the story of the Minoans. Use your dictionary and write a good definition of each to show that you understand the meaning.

1. island: _____

_____

2. textile: _____

_____

3. festival: _____

_____

4. palace: _____

_____

Chapter 1

The Minoans

We have read about some of the first human civilizations. Many of these first civilizations were in a part of the world called the Middle East. The old civilizations of the Sumerians, the Babylonians, and the Egyptians are now gone but historians study the ruins and the writings left behind by these people who lived so long ago. From these ruins and writings we learn much about how people lived in the old lands.

Across the Mediterranean (med-uh-ter-AY-nee-un) Sea, north of Egypt, there was another civilization. It developed on a large **island** (EYE-lund) named Crete (KREET). The people of Crete traded goods with the Egyptians and the Phoenicians (fih-NEESH-uns). They learned writing and the ways of civilization from the Phoenicians and the Egyptians. Because they lived on an **island**, the people of Crete did not have to fight so many wars. They were left alone to develop their civilization in peace.

The people of Crete learned from the Phoenicians to write on clay tablets. Much of this writing has been found on Crete. Recently historians have learned to read some of it. No one today knows how to read all of the writing.

We know some things about Crete and its civilization, however. The people of Crete were ruled by strong kings. The kings were all named Minos (MY-nohss). The people were called Minoans (mih-NO-uns). The Minoans liked **festivals** (FES-tuh-vuls) and shows. They loved bullfights and drew many pictures of them.

The Minoans became fine artists. They made beautiful pottery. Their **textiles** (TEK-stils) were famous all over the ancient world. They used bronze for making tools. They built ships to sail on the Mediterranean Sea.

One of the kings built a **palace** (PAL-us) on the **island** of Crete. It was at a place that historians call Cnossus (k-NAHS-us). The **palace** was very large with many rooms and hallways. Archeologists (ar-kee-OL-uh-jists) have dug in the ruins at Cnossus. They found that the **palace** had a modern water system, a sewer system, and complete bathrooms. The Minoan king had built a fine **palace**.

About 3,400 years ago Crete may have been invaded. The **palace** at Cnossus was destroyed and burned. Historians are not sure who did this. Some think the Greeks who lived to the north may have done it. The Minoans never rebuilt their towns and cities. King Minos never rebuilt his **palace** at Cnossus. No one is sure where the Minoans went. Maybe they were all killed. Maybe some escaped to other lands. Some may have sailed to Greece. Their civilization was gone forever. Dirt covered the **palace** and its water system. Dirt covered broken pottery and bronze tools. Many years later, archeologists would dig the **palace** out of the dust.

There are many old stories about the Minoans which people still read today. In the next chapter, we will learn some of these old stories.

I.

Answer these to help with your reading.

1. What two old civilizations traded with the people of Crete and helped them to progress? _____

_____

2. On what island did the Minoans build their civilization?_____

_____

3. What was the name of the Minoan king? _____

_____

4. Where on Crete was the king's palace? _____

_____

5. On what did the Minoans write?_____

6. What happened to the palace at Cnossus?_____

_____

   When did this happen?_____

_____

II.

Circle True or False.

T   F   1. Crete is an island in the Mediterranean Sea.

T   F   2. The kings on Crete were called Pharaoh.

T   F   3. Historians can read all the Minoan writing.

T   F   4. One of the Minoan kings built a palace at Cnossus.

T   F   5. The palace at Cnossus had a fine water system.

T   F   6. The palace at Cnossus is standing today.

III.   **Use one of the four vocabulary words from the beginning of this chapter to complete each sentence below.**

1. The large house of a ruler is known as a _____ .

2. A piece of land which has water all around it is called an

_____ .

3. A feast or a holiday that occurs each year at the same time is a

_____ .

4. A woven fabric or material is called a _____ .

IV.   **Think about and discuss in class.**

The Minoans liked festivals and shows. We also celebrate (SELL-uh-brayt) festivals and holidays. What are some of the holidays we celebrate?

_____   _____

_____   _____

_____   _____

_____   _____

Which of those you wrote down are religious holidays? _____

_____

Which are very old holidays? _____

_____

How do we celebrate each holiday you listed? _____

_____

When Icarus flew too close to the sun, the wax holding his wings together melted. He fell to his death in the sea.

King Aegeas saw the black sail on Theseus' ship as it returned home. He believed his son was dead.

Ariadne gave Theseus a ball of yarn to help him find his way out of the maze after he had killed the Minotaur.

Getting Ready For Chapter Two

Here are four vocabulary words that are used in the story of the Greek myths about the Minoans. Use your dictionary and write a good definition of each to show that you understand the meaning.

1. myth: _____

_____

2. maze: _____

_____

3. Aegean Sea: _____

_____

4. honor: _____

_____

2

The Minotaur, a man-eating
monster that was half human
and half bull, was kept in a
prison shaped like a maze.

Chapter 2

Greek Myths about the Minoans

The stories in this chapter are Greek stories. They are about the Minoans. Long ago they may have been Minoan stories, but the Greeks took the stories as their own. These stories are **myths** (MITHS). **Myths** are a special kind of story. They tell how people looked at life. Often they explain some practice or belief. Many times **myths** are about some things that actually happened. The stories are so old that no one knows for sure how much in the **myths** actually did happen and how much was added by people later. **Myths** are fun because they show what people believe about life and themselves.

Long ago King Minos had a large monster at Cnossus (k-NAHS-us). The monster had a man's body and the head of a wild bull. It was called the Minotaur (MIN-uh-tor). The Minotaur liked to eat people, so the king had to find a place to lock it away. He asked a man named Daedalus (DED-uh-lus) to build a huge **maze** (MAYZ) at Cnossus. The Minotaur was kept in the **maze**. It could not find its way out. People who went into the **maze** could never find their way out either. They were lost forever.

Every year King Minos ordered the Greek King Aegeas (ee-JEE-us) of Athens (ATH-unz) to send seven young women and seven young men to be fed to the Minotaur. Since the king of Athens feared King Minos, he sent the fourteen young people every year.

King Aegeas had a son named Theseus (THEE-see-us). When Theseus grew up, he decided to go to Cnossus to kill the Minotaur. His father agreed and Theseus got ready to sail for Crete. He told his father that when his ship returned, it would have white sails if the Minotaur had been killed. But if he had failed and was killed, his ship would have black sails. Theseus then sailed to Crete.

At Cnossus Theseus and the daughter of King Minos, named Ariadne (air-ee-AD-nee), fell in love. Ariadne, with the help of Daedalus, decided to aid Theseus. She gave him a large ball of string to take into the **maze**. By unrolling the string as he went, Theseus would be able to find his way back out of the **maze** after he killed the Minotaur.

Theseus killed the Minotaur and found his way out of the **maze**. He took Ariadne with him and sailed for home. In his excitement he forgot to change the sails of his ship to white. His father, King Aegeas, saw the returning ship with black sails. Because he thought his son was dead, King Aegeas jumped from a rock into the Mediterranean Sea and was killed. Theseus then became king of Athens.

From the time of King Aegeas' death, that part of the Mediterranean Sea where he was killed has been called the **Aegean Sea** (uh-JEE-un SEE) in **honor** (ON-er) of him. (See if you can find the **Aegean Sea** on the map on page 1.)

Back in Crete, King Minos had Daedalus and his son Icarus (IK-uh-rus) put into the **maze** for helping Theseus. But Daedalus was too smart for King Minos. He invented wings made from feathers for himself and his son. He put the wings together with wax. Daedalus warned Icarus not to fly too close to the sun because wax melts when it is near heat. Then he and Icarus flew out of the **maze** with no trouble. Icarus liked flying. He went higher and higher. He flew too close to the sun and the wax melted. His wings fell apart and Icarus dropped into the Mediterranean Sea and drowned.

These Greek stories about the Minoans are still enjoyed today. Historians wonder if Daedalus was an inventor who tried to make a flying machine. Maybe Icarus was really a kind of glider. The Mediterranean Sea near Greece is still called the **Aegean Sea**. The old Greek **myth** tells how it came to get that name. The Greeks today still tell these stories. How much of them to believe is up to each reader.

I.   **Answer these to help with your reading.**

1. What was the monster at Cnossus called? _____

_____

2. What did the monster look like? _____

_____

Where did King Minos keep the monster? _____

_____

3. What was King Aegeas forced to send to King Minos each year? _____

_____

4. Who helped Theseus find his way out of the maze? _____

5. Why did King Aegeas jump into the sea and kill himself? _____

_____

6. How did Daedalus and Icarus escape from the maze? _____

_____

7. Why did Icarus fall into the sea? _____

_____

II.

Circle the right word or words to complete the sentences below.

1. The story of the Minotaur is

   a. an Egyptian story   b. a news story   c. a Greek myth

2. The Minotaur was a monster with the head of a

   a. bull   b. dog   c. king

3. The Minotaur was kept in a

   a. cage   b. maze   c. box

4. The maze at Cnossus was built by

   a. Icarus   b. Daedalus   c. Theseus

5. Theseus found his way out of the maze with the help of a

   a. ball of string   b. compass   c. seeing-eye dog

6. Theseus' father was

   a. King Minos   b. Daedalus   c. King Aegeas

7. The part of the Mediterranean where King Aegeas died is

   a. the Icarian Sea   b. North Sea   c. the Aegean Sea

Use one of the four vocabulary words from the beginning of this chapter to complete each of the sentences below.

1. The part of the Mediterranean Sea near Athens is named the

   _____   _____ .

III.

2. Paths or hallways which are built to confuse a person are called a

   _____ .

3. When we show respect to someone who is important, we _____ him or her.

4. An old story telling about people and events that may have happened and which shows how people looked at life is known as a _____ .

IV.   **Think about and enjoy in class.**

Below is a maze for you to find your way through. See if you can go in the right door, find and kill the Minotaur, and find your way out.

The maze in the story of the Minotaur must have been very large. How could such a maze be built? _____

Archeologists think that the palace at Cnossus was so large and had so many hallways that it was like a maze. Maybe the maze at Cnossus was really the palace. Have you ever been in a large building with so many hallways that you felt you were lost in a maze?

The Greeks used wood from their forests to build small ships. They sailed to other lands to trade.

The Greeks first learned from the Minoans how to make pottery. Often the Greeks drew pictures on their pots to show scenes from myths.

The Greek farmers raised grapes for wine and olives for oil.

3 Getting Ready For Chapter Three

Here are three vocabulary words that are used in the story of the Greeks and Greece. Use your dictionary and write a good definition of each to show that you understand the meaning.

1. city-state: _____

_____

2. united: _____

_____

3. language: _____

_____

Many of the early Greeks
farmed and tended sheep.

Chapter

3

The Greeks and Greece

To the north of the island of Crete are many small islands and the coast of Europe (YUR-up). This part of the Mediterranean Sea is called the Aegean Sea, and the land on its coast is called Greece. Greece is a small country. People have lived there for many thousands of years. But at the time the Minoans built their civilization on Crete, Greece was only a wild country with many mountains and deep valleys.

Some Minoans lived in Greece and traded with the Greeks. Many of these Greeks were small farmers and shepherds. Greek valleys were green and there were many olive trees and grapevines. The olives were used for their oil and the grapes were made into wine. Over many years the Greeks began to learn the civilized ways of the Minoans. They learned to write and they saw some of the beautiful drawings and pottery the Minoans made. They began to make some pottery and statues and drawings of their own.

Although their coast is rough (RUFF), it has many small harbors and the people who lived in Greece became good sailors. They built strong ships from the wood that grew in forests on Greek mountains. The Greeks sailed to other lands and islands and conquered the people on many of them. They started several Greek colonies. Some historians believe that when the great palace of King Minos at Cnossus was destroyed completely around 1400 B.C., it may have been the Greeks who did this.

The Greeks lived in small communities called **city-states**. This happened partly because in Greece the mountains divide the country into small valleys. A group of people lived in each of these small valleys. The people living within a valley knew each other. They worked and talked and did things they enjoyed together. They decided on their own laws and rules. They did not have one ruler make decisions for everyone. Instead, they decided together how they would live. They called this way of living and ruling themselves a **city-state**. The Greeks believed these **city-states** were the best way for people to live because each group governed itself.

The **city-states** in Greece were not **united** (yoo-NITE-ud) into one nation like Egypt or Babylonia. Often they even fought with each other. But there were many things that kept the Greeks together. They were all of the same race (RAYSS). They all spoke the same **language** (LANG-gwij). They all knew the same old stories and myths, and they had the same gods.

I.   **Answer these to help with your reading.**

1. Name two trees or plants that grow in Greece.

   a. _____

   b. _____

2. Who helped the Greeks become civilized? _____

_____

3. Tell some things people in a Greek city-state did together. _____

_____

_____

4. What are three things that kept the Greek people together?

   a. _____

   b. _____

   c. _____

II.   **Circle the right word or words to complete each sentence below.**

1. The part of Europe near the Aegean Sea is called

   a. Minos   b. island   c. Greece

2. The country called Greece is

   a. small   b. large   c. low

3. The Greeks made grapes into

   a. water   b. oil   c. wine

4. The Greeks lived in

   a. farms   b. city-states   c. canals

III.   **Circle True or False.**

   T   F   1. The Mediterranean Sea near Greece is called the Aegean Sea.

T F 2. The Greeks learned civilized ways from the Babylonians.

T F 3. The city-states of Greece were united.

T F 4. The Greeks spoke many languages.

IV.

Use one of the three vocabulary words from the beginning of this chapter to complete each of the sentences below.

1. When the members of a group act together as one, we say they

   are _____ .

2. The words used and understood by a people are their _____ .

3. A city and the land around it which rules itself, as in ancient Greece, make

   up a _____ .

V.

Think about and discuss in class.

The Greeks made olive oil from the olives that grew on their land.

What kind of plant do olives grow on? _____

How do you suppose olives are turned into oil? _____

_____

_____

What is olive oil used for? _____

_____

The Greeks made wine from the grapes which grew on the hillsides. How is

wine made from grapes? _____

_____

_____

_____

_____

The Greeks loved to hear how, in early times, their people had conquered the city of Troy. The Greek soldiers could not batter down Troy's strong walls, so they had used a trick to make the Trojans open the gates for them. Chapter Four tells what the trick was.

Odysseus and his men escaped from the Cyclops, the giant with only one eye, by blinding him while he slept.

The blind storyteller Homer is famous for his two stories, the *Iliad* and the *Odyssey*.

4 Getting Ready For Chapter Four

Here are five vocabulary words that are used in the story of the *Iliad* and the *Odyssey*. Use your dictionary and write a good definition of each to show that you understand the meaning.

1. bard: _____

_____

2. legend: _____

_____

3. *Iliad*: _____

_____

4. *Odyssey*: _____

_____

5. literature: _____

_____

Chapter 4 The *Iliad* and the *Odyssey*

The Greek people were held together by their language as well as by their myths and stories. The myths and stories were often about great heroes and gods. We have read the myths about Theseus and the Minotaur and of Daedalus and Icarus. These were two of the Greeks' favorite (FAYV-u-rut) stories.

The most famous and best-loved stories of the Greeks were the stories by Homer. Homer's stories are very old. They were made up before the Greeks learned how to write. Historians believe that Homer was a blind storyteller. He went from town to town telling his stories to the people. Historians believe that Homer might even have sung his stories and played music, too. Storytellers such as Homer were called **bards** (BARDS).

Homer's stories were old **legends** (LEJ-unds) about the Greek heroes in the war with Troy. The Greeks called the city of Troy Ilium (ILL-ee-um). Homer's story of the Trojan (TRO-jun) War is called the *Iliad* (ILL-ee-ud). It is one of the most famous stories ever told. After the Greeks learned to write, they put the *Iliad* into writing. Today it is read and enjoyed by many people.

The *Iliad* tells how the Trojan War began. Paris, son of the king of Troy, fell in love with Helen, the wife of a Greek king. Paris took Helen to Troy. The Greeks were very angry and attacked Troy to get Helen back. The Greeks fought (FAWT) with the Trojans for ten years. Homer's story covers forty days in the tenth year of the war.

It tells the story of Achilles (uh-KILL-eez), the greatest Greek warrior, who refused to fight any more because he was angry at the other warriors. Because he stopped fighting, the Trojans were able to win many battles. In one battle, Hector, the greatest Trojan warrior, killed Achilles' best friend. This made Achilles begin fighting again. He killed Hector, and the Greeks began to win the war.

One of the Greek heroes of the Trojan War was Odysseus (o-DIS-ee-us), often called Ulysses (yoo-LISS-ees). Odysseus built a famous wooden horse that the Greeks used to fool the Trojans. The Greeks built the wooden horse so large that many men could hide inside. The Trojans took the horse inside the walls of their city because they thought it was a gift from the Greeks. The Greeks inside the horse waited until night and then climbed out, attacked and killed the surprised Trojans, and won the war.

After the war, Odysseus sailed for home. He had much trouble getting back to Greece. It took him ten years to get home. He had many adventures on the way. He had to fight a one-eyed giant called the Cyclops (SY-klops). Homer told about this and other adventures in a second story. Homer's story of Odysseus', or Ulysses', trip home is named the *Odyssey* (OD-uh-see). Homer's two stories are part of the world's great **literature** (LIT-uh-rah-chur).

I. **Answer these to help with your reading.**

1. What was the name of the man who wrote some of the most famous and best-loved Greek stories?_____

2. Why were the people of ancient Greece glad to listen to an exciting story told by a storyteller?_____

3. What are the names of Homer's two famous stories?_____

_____

4. How long did the Greeks fight the Trojans? _____
   How long did it take Odysseus to reach his home in Greece?_____

5. What did Odysseus build to trick the Trojans?_____

_____

6. By what other name do we know Odysseus?_____

_____

II. **Circle the right word or words to complete each sentence below.**

1. The most famous Greek stories were told by Homer, a bard who was

   a. lame   b. blind   c. Egyptian

2. The Greeks called the city of Troy

   a. Ilium   b. Greece   c. Babylon

3. The Trojan who took Helen to Troy was

   a. Ulysses   b. Theseus   c. Paris

4. Odysseus fought a giant who had only one

   a. ear   b. arm   c. eye

5. The wooden horse, called the Trojan horse, was built by

    a. Paris   b. Odysseus   c. the Trojans

III.   **Use one of the five vocabulary words from the beginning of this chapter to complete each of the sentences below.**

1. Writings that continue to be read for hundreds of years because of their ideas and their way of saying these ideas are called _____ .

2. Homer's great story of the Trojan War is named the _____ .

3. Old stories of life in the past, which many people have believed, are called _____ .

4. A poet who writes or sings of heroes and their deeds is known as a _____ .

5. Homer's story of Odysseus and his trip back to Greece is named the _____ .

IV.   **Think about and discuss in class.**

You and your classmates may have read stories from the *Iliad* or the *Odyssey*. Maybe you have read other stories about Greek heroes, too. Hercules (HER-kyoo-leez) was a great Greek hero. So was Achilles. Do you remember reading about Jason and the Golden Fleece? That too is an old Greek story. Maybe your teacher could retell one or two of these stories. Better yet, maybe someone in your class could help tell the story.

What did Hercules do? _____

_____

_____

How did Odysseus stop the Cyclops? _____

How did Jason get the Golden Fleece? _____

_____

In one of Aesop's fables, a greedy man discovers that the goose he owns lays golden eggs.

A Black Storyteller of Greece

A man named Aesop (EE-sop) became one of the most famous storytellers of ancient Greece. It is not known exactly where or when Aesop was born. When telling of him, ancient Greeks said only that he lived in Greece, was a slave from Asia, and that his skin was black. Aesop lived and told his stories more than five hundred years before the birth of Christ.

Aesop's stories are called "fables." A fable is a story that is made up to teach a lesson. Fables are often about animals who can talk. The things the animals say teach people lessons about life. They show that liking yourself too much, being too greedy, and being too proud are not good.

Aesop's fables were very popular in ancient Greece and they are still popular today. They are read in countries all over the world. You may have read some of Aesop's fables yourself. Here are two of them.

I. THE FOX AND THE CROW — A Crow took a piece of cheese from the window of a house. The Crow flew high into a tree to eat the cheese. A Fox who saw the Crow with the cheese sat down by the tree. The Fox began to compliment the Crow on her beauty. The Fox told her how beautiful her feathers were and how graceful her body was shaped. "I'll bet you have a beautiful voice," the Fox said. The Crow was so pleased by the compliments that she could not resist singing a song for the Fox. But when she began to sing, the cheese dropped from her mouth. This was just what the Fox wanted. He caught the cheese as it dropped and ate it up. As he trotted away he laughed to himself about how easy it was to get the cheese away from the Crow.

II. THE GOOSE THAT LAID THE GOLDEN EGGS — A man owned a goose which laid a golden egg for him every day. But, being greedy, the man was not satisfied with just one golden egg a day. He decided to take his whole treasure at once. Killing the goose, the man cut her open to remove the golden eggs. But all he found was what one would find in any goose. For wanting too much, he had nothing.

To keep Zeus from being swallowed by his father, his mother gave him to two nymphs, who cared for him and fed him goat's milk.

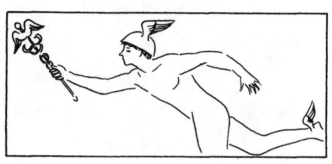

Hermes was the messenger of the gods. He had wings on his cap and on his shoes so he could carry messages quickly. Today, some businesses which pride themselves on their speed use a picture of Hermes to advertise.

5 Getting Ready For Chapter Five

Here are two vocabulary words that are used in the story of the Greek gods and goddesses. Use your dictionary and write a good definition of each to show that you understand the meaning.

1. nymphs: _____

_____

2. chariot: _____

_____

The Greeks told a strange story of how Athena, a favorite goddess of theirs, was born. They said that her father, Zeus, had a headache. To cure it, Zeus had his head split open by an ax. Then out stepped Athena, already grown and completely dressed.

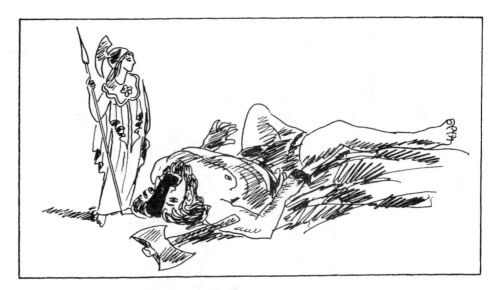

The Greeks built many temples to honor their gods and goddesses.

Chapter 5

The Greek Gods and Goddesses

The Greeks had many gods and goddesses who they believed controlled the lives of humans. Apollo was the god of light. He was the sun god. Every day, Apollo drove his **chariot** (CHAIR-ee-ut), the sun, across the sky. Ares (AIR-eez) was the god of war. Hermes (HER-meez) was the god of travelers, leading them away from danger. He was also the messenger of Zeus (ZOOSS). Zeus was the greatest of the Greek gods. He was obeyed (o-BAYD) by all the other gods and goddesses.

The Greeks liked to tell stories about Zeus. Their stories say that Zeus was born on a mountain in Crete. His father always swallowed his children while they were babies because he was afraid they would grow up to be more powerful than he. To save Zeus, his mother wrapped a large stone in a blanket. Zeus' father swallowed the stone thinking it was his child. Then Zeus' mother gave him to a pair of **nymphs** (NIMFS), who cared for him. He was fed on the milk of a goat.

When Zeus was full grown, he became more powerful than his father. He punished his father by sending him to the far ends of the earth. Zeus then fought the other gods in the sky until he had put them all in chains and buried them in the earth. Zeus became the most powerful god of all.

Many of the Greek stories about Zeus are about his adventures with women. He was married to Hera (HEER-uh). Hera often became upset about Zeus and his other women. Then there was trouble in the skies! The Greeks used these stories to explain thunder and storms. They liked to believe that Hera and Zeus were having another fight.

The Greeks especially liked the goddess Athena (uh-THEE-nah). The Greek city of Athens was named for her. She was a daughter of Zeus. According to legend, when Metis, the mother of Athena, was about to have a child, Zeus was worried that the child would become more powerful than he. He swallowed Metis, and shortly after that, he had a bad headache. To cure this, his head was split open with a bronze ax. Out of his head popped his daughter, Athena, fully grown, fully dressed, and with a long spear. Athena became Zeus' favorite daughter, but she did not always obey him.

The Greeks built temples for their gods and goddesses and statues (STACH-oos) too. They had stories about them all. These stories are still read today. Many can be found in the school library. The class might enjoy reading more of these old Greek stories.

I. Answer these to help with your reading.

1. Who was the greatest of the Greek gods? _____

   Where was he born? _____

2. To whom was Zeus married? _____

3. For which goddess was the city of Athens named? _____

   _____

4. Who was the Greek sun god? _____

5. Which god was the messenger of Zeus? _____

6. What was the name of the god of war? _____

II. Circle the right word or words to complete the sentences below.

1. The ruler of all the Greek gods and goddesses was

   a. Homer   b. Apollo   c. Zeus

2. Zeus was born

   a. on Crete   b. in Athens   c. in Egypt

3. When Zeus was a baby, he was fed

   a. by a monster   b. with a bottle   c. on the milk of a goat

4. Zeus was married to

   a. Athena   b. Hera   c. a nymph

5. Zeus' favorite daughter was

   a. Hera   b. a nymph   c. Athena

6. Apollo drove a chariot which was

   a. the moon   b. the earth   c. the sun

7. The god who kept travelers from danger was

   a. Zeus   b. Hermes   c. Apollo

8. For their gods and goddesses, the Greeks built many

    a. temples and statues   b. cities and towns   c. churches

III.

Circle True or False.

T F 1. The Greeks believed the gods and goddesses controlled the lives of humans.

T F 2. Zeus' mother tricked his father into swallowing a stone.

T F 3. Zeus' mother took care of him until he grew up.

T F 4. The Greeks had only one god.

T F 5. Athena popped out of her father's head.

T F 6. Athena did not always obey Zeus.

IV.

Use one of the two vocabulary words from the beginning of this chapter to complete each of the sentences below.

1. An ancient two-wheeled cart used for wars and races was known as

    a _____ .

2. In Greek myths, beautiful maidens who were goddesses of nature and lived

    in the mountains and forests were called _____ .

V.

Think about and discuss in class.

Choose one person in the class to go to the school library and get several books with stories of Greek gods and goddesses. The librarian will know where these books are in the library. Have your teacher read a few stories to the class. Write the names of the books on the lines below. Then if you would like, you can find them in the library and read more stories for yourself.

_____

_____

_____

_____

A Review of Vocabulary Words

Match the words in Column A with the correct definitions in Column B. Draw lines to the right definitions. When everyone is finished, discuss the words and their meanings to be sure each person has them right.

Column A	Column B
the *Iliad* •	• the large house of a ruler
chariot •	• story of Odysseus or Ulysses
legends •	• stories that tell how people looked at life
Aegean Sea •	• the great writings of a country
palace •	• showing respect for an important person
textiles •	• story of the Trojan war
bard •	• old stories of life in the past
the *Odyssey* •	• acting together as one
honor •	• a poet or storyteller
literature •	• Mediterranean Sea near Athens
united •	• woven fabrics or materials
myths •	• two-wheeled horse-drawn cart

When the Greeks had won the battle at Marathon, they sent a runner twenty-six miles to Athens to tell the good news. This same distance is the length of the marathon race run in the Olympic Games today.

6

Getting Ready For Chapter Six

Here are three vocabulary words that are used in the story of the Persian Wars. Use your dictionary and write a good definition of each to show that you understand the meaning.

1. empire: _____

_____

2. marathon: _____

_____

3. celebrate: _____

_____

Xerxes sat on a high hill to watch the sea battle between his ships and the navy of the Greeks. He was sure his huge fleet would win.

When the Greeks fought the Persians on the plain of Marathon, they were out-numbered two to one. But by planning the battle carefully, the Greeks were able to beat the Persians.

Chapter 6

The Persian Wars

The Greek lands were not always safe from the armies of other countries. Greece was almost conquered by a people from the East. These people were the Persians (PER-zhuns), who came from east of Babylon. They had already built a great **empire** (EM-pyr) around their land of Persia (PER-zhuh). The Persians had a great king named Darius (duh-RY-us). Darius wanted to conquer Greece and add it to his **empire**.

Persia had millions of soldiers and many riches. The Greek city-states were poor and small when compared to Persia. And no one could be sure the city-states would ever unite (yoo-NYT) to fight against Darius. Things did not look good for the Greeks when the Persian army began invading some Greek colonies in Asia.

The Greeks sent a small army to help protect some of their colonies. They won a battle against Darius and made him very angry. He said he would kill every Greek in the world. About 490 B.C. Darius sent his army to Greece by ship. They landed on a plain called **Marathon** (MAIR-uh-thon). **Marathon** is only twenty-six miles from Athens. Athens sent for help from the other city-states. Only one city would help, and it sent just one thousand men. The Greeks prepared to fight the Persians.

At **Marathon** the Greeks fought one of the most famous battles in history. The Persians outnumbered them two to one. But the Greeks planned their defense so well they were able to overpower the Persians. At the end of the battle the Persians had to run to their ships. The Greeks sent a fast runner to Athens to tell the good news. The runner ran twenty-six miles to tell of the victory. To this day there is an event in the Olympic (o-LIM-pik) Games to **celebrate** (SELL-uh-brayt) this victory. It is called a **marathon**, and it is a twenty-six-mile-long race.

The Persian Wars did not end with **Marathon**. Ten years later the Persians had a new king, Xerxes (ZERK-seez). Xerxes wanted to conquer Greece too. He attacked with an army and a huge fleet of ships. The Greeks tried hard to stop the Persians. They did not want to be ruled by any king. Many Greek people died to keep Greece free from outsiders. But the army of Xerxes moved into Athens. The city was destroyed.

The Greeks fled from Athens to an island nearby named Salamis (SAL-ah-muss). Xerxes sent his army there in ships. He sat on a high hill to watch the Persians kill all the Greeks. The Greeks' warships were waiting near a small bay at Salamis. The Persian fleet seemed to have them trapped. But the Greeks had a plan. They made the Persians think they were retreating (ree-TREET-ing). The Persians sailed into the narrow bay to chase them. Then the Greek ships turned around and attacked. The Persians could not get back out of the narrow bay quickly. They had so many ships that there was no room to move! The Greek ships and soldiers put up a good fight, and by the end of the day the Persian fleet was beaten. Xerxes came down from his hill and took his army back to Persia. Greece had been saved.

If the Persians had won their war against Greece, the Greeks would never have had the chance to become a great people. They would have been slaves to the Persians. The Greek gifts to civilization which we will read about in the next chapters might never have happened.

I. **Answer these to help with your reading.**

1. What was the name of the Persian king who wanted to kill every Greek in

   the world? _____

2. On what plain did the Greeks win the battle against Darius' army? _____

   _____

   How far from Athens is this plain?_____

3. How is the victory at Marathon celebrated even today? _____

   _____

   _____

4. Who was the second Persian king to attack the Greeks?_____

   _____

5. To what island did the Greeks go to escape the Persians? _____

   _____

6. What would have happened to the Greeks if they had lost the battle to the

   Persians? _____

   _____

   _____

II. **Circle the right word or words to complete the sentences below.**

1. Persia was east of

   a. Babylon   b. Asia   c. China

2. The Persian king who hated all Greeks was

   a. Zeus   b. Marathon   c. Darius

3. The Greek city-states would not

   a. sing   b. unite   c. talk to each other

4. Darius was defeated at the plain of

   a. Greece   b. Crete   c. Marathon

5. A marathon race is still

   a. twenty-six miles   b. one hundred miles   c. too short

6. Xerxes' army destroyed the Greek city of

   a. Salamis   b. Athens   c. Cnossus

7. The Greeks fought the Persians at Salamis

   a. on horses   b. on foot   c. in ships

III. **Circle True or False.**

T   F   1. The Greeks were almost conquered by the Persians.

T   F   2. The Greeks had more soldiers and wealth than the Persians.

T   F   3. The Greek city-states always united in times of trouble.

T   F   4. The Greeks defeated the Persians in a sea battle at Salamis.

IV. **Use one of the three vocabulary words from the beginning of this chapter to complete each of the sentences below.**

1. A twenty-six-mile-long race is called a _____ .

2. A large area of land with many people under one ruler is known as an _____ .

3. To honor or observe with special activities is to _____ .

33

The Queen Who Fought at Salamis

When Xerxes prepared to attack Greece, many other rulers from Asia decided to join him. Each ruler brought an army or ships to be used in the battles led by Xerxes. One of these rulers was a woman named Artemisia (ar-tem-EE-zee-uh). She was the queen of Halicarnassus (hal-ah-kar-NASS-us).

Artemisia brought five ships and was one of the captains in the sea battle at Salamis. Legend says that, of all his captains, only Artemisia told Xerxes not to fight the Greeks in ships in that bay. She knew that the mouth of the bay was narrow. If they were attacked by the Greeks inside the bay, the Persians would not be able to escape quickly. Xerxes did not listen to Artemisia.

Artemisia is said to have fought bravely at the bay of Salamis. When the Persians were losing, she was asked by Xerxes what should be done. She told Xerxes to go back to Persia. This time Xerxes listened to his captain. He even trusted his children to her care. He asked her to return the children to Asia. Artemisia returned to Halicarnassus where she remained queen until her death.

Greek women spent much of their time in the home spinning wool, weaving textiles, caring for the children and directing the work of the slaves. One task that took them outside was bringing water to the house from fountains that were on the street corners.

On the Acropolis, a high hill overlooking Athens, the Greeks built many beautiful marble temples for their gods and goddesses.

7 Getting Ready For Chapter Seven

Here are four vocabulary words that are used in the story of the Greeks rebuilding Athens. Use your dictionary and write a good definition of each to show that you understand the meaning.

1. agora:_____

_____

2. gossip: _____

_____

3. Acropolis: _____

_____

4. Parthenon:_____

_____

The agora was the meeting place in Athens. People gathered here to talk, to shop, and to trade goods.

The Parthenon once housed a statue of the goddess Athena. The statue is gone now, but historians know that it stood thirty-nine feet tall and was made from ivory decorated with gold.

After 2,400 years, the Parthenon is still standing and is thought to be one of the world's most beautiful buildings.

Chapter 7

The Greeks Rebuild Athens

After the defeat of the Persians, the Greeks moved back to their city of Athens. It was in ruins. The Greeks took many years to rebuild their city. They made Athens a city with the most beautiful buildings in all Greece.

Athens was never a big city. The people lived in brick houses on crowded streets. There were no sewers or water pipes in Athens. Water came from fountains at the street corners and was carried to the houses in large water jars. Most houses had slaves to do the hard work. The women took care of running the house. They did things like spinning wool and weaving textiles for clothing and rugs and they prepared food for cooking. They cared for the sick, raised the children, and kept track of the money. Women did not leave the home often.

In the center of Athens was the marketplace. The Greeks called it the **agora** (AG-u-ruh). **Agora** means "meeting place" and that is what the market was. Most of the men of Athens spent the day there. Government buildings were near the **agora**. Also near the **agora** were small factories and stores. They made and sold beautiful jars, bowls, cups, and plates. There were also furniture stores and wine shops. For the men, there were barber shops too.

The men of Athens met every day at the **agora** and talked. They talked of the latest news and **gossip** (GOSS-up). They argued (AR-gyood) over prices. Sometimes they bought and sold slaves. At noon the market closed and all the men went to an open-air theater (THEE-ut-ur). Here they met to make their laws. Everyone had the right to go to these meetings, but neither women nor slaves had the right to vote. Anyone could speak at the meeting, but if one was a poor speaker, the crowd would throw trash and olive pits at him. The most important men in Athens were those who were the best speakers.

The Greeks built their most beautiful buildings on a high hill called the **Acropolis** (uh-KROP-uh-luss). They built them of marble. The largest building on the **Acropolis** was a temple to Athena, the goddess for whom the city was named. Her temple was called the **Parthenon** (PAR-thuh-non). Inside the **Parthenon** was a statue of Athena that was thirty-nine feet tall. Many people today think that the **Parthenon** is one of the most beautiful buildings ever built.

There were other temples and statues on the **Acropolis**. The **Acropolis** was the showplace of Athens. Strangers came to visit it by the thousands. The **Acropolis** became the center of Athens, and Athens became the center of the civilized world.

The Greek way of building has been copied (KOP-eed) all over the world. In our country there are many buildings like those of ancient Athens. The Lincoln Memorial in Washington is much like the **Parthenon**. In Nashville, Tennessee, there is a building which is an exact copy of the **Parthenon**.

I.   **Answer these to help with your reading.**

1. Where did the people of Athens get water for their homes? _____

_____

2. Where did most of the men of Athens spend their day? _____

_____

What did Greek women do during the day? _____

_____

_____

3. What does the Greek word "agora" mean? _____

4. In the afternoon, where did Greek men go? _____

What was done at these meetings? _____

_____

5. How did the people at the meetings treat a poor speaker? _____

_____

6. Where did the Greeks build their most beautiful buildings? _____

_____

7. Where can one find buildings built in the Greek way in the United States

today? _____

_____

_____

II. **Circle True or False.**

T F 1. Athens was never a big city.

T F 2. Athens had a fine water system and sewers.

T F 3. The "agora" was a Greek temple.

T F 4. The most important men in Athens were good speakers.

T F 5. The Parthenon was a temple to honor Zeus.

T F 6. Buildings like those on the Acropolis at Athens have been copied all over the world.

III. **Use one of the four vocabulary words from the beginning of this chapter to complete each sentence below.**

1. The temple to Athena, often described as one of the most beautiful ever built, is named the _____ .

2. The high hill above Athens on which the Greeks built temples is called the _____ .

3. Idle chatter about people, which cannot be proved, is called _____ .

4. In Athens the marketplace was known as the _____ .

IV. **Think about and discuss in class.**

Find the word "architecture" in your dictionary. Write its meaning.

_____

_____

_____

_____

The Greeks had their own architecture (AR-kuh-tek-chur) and it is very famous. Even today buildings in most cities have parts that are copied from the Greeks. The Greeks liked to build with columns (KOL-ums). The top part of each column is called the capital, and it carries the weight of the roof above it. The Greeks had three kinds of capitals on top of their columns. Here is a drawing of each.

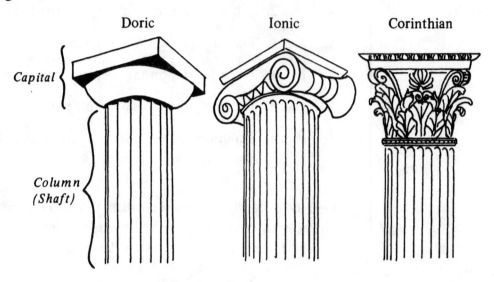

Doric   Ionic   Corinthian

Capital

Column (Shaft)

On page 36 is a drawing of the Parthenon on the Acropolis. What kind of

capitals are on its columns? _____

This kind was the Greeks' favorite capital. Write the names of the other two kinds of capitals.

1. _____

2. _____

On the way home from school today, look for some columns with capitals like those the Greeks used. Old stores or banks often have them. Look at some of the buildings near where you live. Maybe some of them have Greek columns. Perhaps your classmates know where some buildings with columns and capitals are. You might even try to draw them after school. Decide what kind of column and capital you have seen. Then label your drawing.

Aristotle was a Greek philosopher who wrote about many things. Some of his writings deal with the good and bad parts of government.

Socrates was a great Greek thinker. He taught his students by asking them questions. He wanted his students to think about their actions.

8

Getting Ready For Chapter Eight

Here are five vocabulary words that are used in the story of five famous Greek men. Use your dictionary and write a good definition of each to show that you understand the meaning.

1. philosophy: _____

_____

2. physics: _____

_____

3. lever: _____

_____

4. oath: _____

_____

5. philosopher: _____

_____

Archimedes invented a machine that would make water flow up a tube when someone turned a crank. It could be used to irrigate fields. He also studied how a lever can make a small force move a large weight.

One of the first people to treat disease with scientific methods was Hippocrates. He taught these methods to his students. Doctors today swear to an oath which Hippocrates wrote thousands of years ago.

Chapter 8

Five Famous Greeks

We have read that the Greeks were a very gifted people. Their ideas and discoveries helped people who lived after them. Among the ancient Greeks, there were many that were famous. Today we will read about five Greeks who helped people progress in science, medicine (MED-uh-sun), and **philosophy** (fuh-LOSS-uh-fee).

One famous man of Greece was Archimedes (ark-uh-MEED-eez). Archimedes loved math and science. He discovered many of the laws of **physics** (FIZ-iks) which we still use today. It is said that he used a reflecting mirror and the sun to set enemy ships on fire while they were still far from the shore. Archimedes understood the way a **lever** (LEV-er) works. He once said, "Give me a place to put my **lever** and I will move the earth." Archimedes invented a machine to lift water for irrigation. His machine is still used in many places today. Archimedes advanced science for all humankind.

Hippocrates (hip-POK-rah-teez) was a Greek doctor. Historians call him the "Father of Medicine." Not much is known about Hippocrates' life. He traveled widely and taught medicine wherever he went. He was the first man to treat disease (diz-EEZ) with scientific methods. He taught his students to notice all the symptoms of the sick person and to compare these to other cases they had seen. Then they could decide how best to treat the illness.

Doctors through the ages have honored the name of Hippocrates. Today doctors all swear to an **oath** (OHTH) which Hippocrates wrote thousands of years ago. It is called the Hippocratic (hip-uh-KRAT-ic) **oath** and it says that the doctor will work for the good of the sick and that the doctor will be honest and not gossip about the sick. You may have seen this **oath** printed and hanging on the wall of a doctor's office.

Ancient Greece produced many **philosophers** (fuh-LOSS-uh-fers), but three were especially famous. They were Socrates (SOK-ruh-tees), Plato (PLAYT-o) and Aristotle (AIR-uh-stot-ul). Of these three, Socrates was the most important. He is often called one of the world's greatest thinkers. Socrates himself never wrote any books. One of his students, Plato, wrote down what Socrates said.

Socrates taught many young Greeks his ideas. He taught his pupils by asking questions. He never gave answers. When his students answered unwisely, Socrates would continue asking questions until they discovered answers for themselves. He believed that each person is good. To Socrates the only evil was to live without thinking about and examining one's actions. Socrates did not believe some of the stories told about the Greek gods. He also taught his students to question the government. Because he encouraged his students to question and to think about things, Socrates made people angry. He was arrested and sentenced to death. The method of killing criminals in those days was poison. In 399 B.C., or about 2,400 years ago, Socrates drank his cup of poison and died.

Socrates' students continued his beliefs. His most famous student was Plato. Plato wrote down the words of Socrates. He also was a great thinker himself. Plato began a school for young Greek men. Plato tried to plan a perfect way of life for all people. He was the first person to try to do this.

Plato's most famous student was Aristotle. Aristotle became a teacher and a writer. He wrote about the good and the bad parts of governments, but he did not try to set up a perfect plan. His thinking, as well as that of Plato and Socrates, is studied for what can be learned from it today. People still seek the wisdom (WIZ-dum) of the ancient Greeks.

I.   Answer these to help with your reading.

1. Write the names of the five people of Greece you have just read about.

    a. _____

    b. _____

    c. _____

    d. _____

    e. _____

2. Tell one thing Archimedes did or invented. _____

_____

3. What do historians call Hippocrates? _____

_____

4. Who wrote the oath that doctors today all swear to? _____

_____

Tell some things it says. _____

_____

5. Who was the most important Greek philosopher? _____

6. How did Socrates die? _____

7. Who wrote down Socrates' ideas? _____

8. Tell one idea that Socrates believed. _____

_____

II.   **Circle the right word or words to complete the following sentences.**

1. Archimedes loved

    a. singing and dancing   b. math and science   c. to talk

2. Hippocrates was a

    a. thinker   b. writer   c. doctor

3. Hippocrates' oath is still taken by

    a. doctors   b. teachers   c. presidents

4. Socrates died by

    a. eating too much   b. the sword   c. drinking poison

5. Socrates' ideas were written down by

    a. his wife   b. Plato   c. a scribe

6. To Socrates the only evil was

    a. drinking   b. stealing   c. living without
                                              thinking about
                                              your actions

7. Plato's most famous student was

    a. Aristotle   b. Socrates   c. Hippocrates

III. **Use one of the five vocabulary words from the beginning of this chapter to complete each of the sentences below.**

1. A person who studies philosophy and thinks about life is a

   _____ .

2. A simple tool used to pry something is called a _____ .

3. The study of life and the love of wisdom is known as _____ .

4. The study of the physical world and natural science is _____ .

5. A solemn promise is an _____ .

IV. **Think about and discuss in class.**

Today's chapter is about five people who are remembered after more than two thousand years.

Why do you think they have been remembered? _____

_____

What people of today do you think might be remembered two thousand or

even just two hundred years from now? _____

_____

Think of the famous men and women you hear about on TV or that you read about in books, newspapers, or magazines. Can you list any names?

_____   _____

_____   _____

Compare the list of names you have written with those of your classmates. See if together your class can make a good list of some great people.

Tell why you consider the person "great." _____

_____

Are there any qualities that all or most great people have? _____

_____

Sappho, a great poet living on an island near Greece, taught writing and art to young women.

The Woman Poet of Greece

The greatest woman to write poetry in Greece was named Sappho (SAF-oh). She wrote poems about love and about the beauty of nature. Only a few of her complete poems have been saved. But many lines from her poetry appear in the works of ancient authors.

Little is known about Sappho's life. It is believed she was born into a rich family about six hundred years before the birth of Christ. She was born on one of the islands in the Aegean Sea. She and her family were forced to leave their home when there was trouble in the government. Sappho lived the rest of her life in a Greek colony. She was one of the few women who taught art and writing. She wrote a poem for each of her students when they left the school. Nothing is known about how or when Sappho died.

Here is a poem written by Sappho:

EVENING
Evening, you bring all things home;
    All that the long day has scattered wide.
The sheep, the goat, back to the welcome flock;
    You bring the child, too, to its mother's side.

Greek plays entertained the people. The plays were given in large open-air theaters. Rows of seats curved around the stage the way a grandstand curves around a baseball field.

Greek athletes enjoyed competing in the Olympic Games, which were held every four years. They threw the discus, ran races, and boxed or wrestled. At that time, only men could compete.

Getting Ready For Chapter Nine

Here are five vocabulary words that are used in the story of the theater and the Olympic Games. Use your dictionary and write a good definition of each to show that you understand the meaning.

1. entertain: _____

_____

2. drama: _____

_____

3. responsible: _____

_____

4. violence: _____

_____

5. athlete: _____

_____

Chapter 9 The Theater and the Olympic Games

The Greeks liked to be **entertained** (ent-ur-TAYND) and loved to listen to stories. We have already read about some of the stories the Greeks liked. We have also read about Homer's two great stories, the *Iliad* and the *Odyssey*. Traveling bards **entertained** the people in the marketplace with these old stories.

The Greek people also developed other kinds of entertainment. One of the greatest things the Greeks gave humankind was the theater, or **drama** (DRAHM-uh). The people of Greece loved to go to the theater to see a good play. The Greeks invented **drama** or plays and built large open-air places where the people could sit while watching them. Greek writers wrote many fine plays for the people to enjoy. Only a few of these plays exist in written form today. Most were lost over the thousands of years since the time of the Greeks.

The Greek people liked to see plays about their gods and their rulers. In the plays the gods held people, even rulers, **responsible** (ree-SPON-suh-bul) for their actions. The gods punished people who were bad. Usually the plays did not end happily. The actors wore masks to show if they were happy or sad. Greek plays had less action on stage than many modern plays. Instead, the actors talked and described what was supposed to be taking place. Greek plays may seem dull today. This is because they often tell ideas rather than show actions. We are used to seeing blood and **violence** (VY-uh-lenss) in our entertainment. The Greeks did not show these things directly in their plays.

Plays were given in Greece as part of a celebration, usually in the spring or the fall. Three plays were given in a row, and often they were about the same people or the same family. The Greek people liked laughing and crying with the characters in the play. Prizes were given to the writers of the best plays.

The Greeks were also **entertained** at the Olympic Games. Once every four years **athletes** (ATH-leets) from all over Greece met to play in the Olympic Games. The games were held in honor of the god Zeus. Only men could compete. Athletes jumped, threw, and ran for prizes. The usual events included a short race of about two hundred yards and a long race of about one and one-half miles. Then the athletes threw the discus (DIS-kus) and the javelin (JAV-uh-lun), a long spear. There was wrestling and boxing too. The winning **athletes** were given many honors.

The Olympic Games were the one thing that usually united the Greeks. Historians say the first games were held in 776 B.C. That was more than 2,775 years ago.

Even now, **athletes** meet every four years to compete in the Olympic Games. Now women and men from all over the world, not just Greece, take part. Modern sports events have been added to the games. There is swimming and skiing (SKEE-ing) and diving too. People hope the games will help unite the people of the world the way they united the Greeks.

I. **Answer these to help with your reading.**

1. Tell one of the greatest things the Greeks gave humankind. _____

_____

2. How many Greek plays still exist today? _____

3. What subjects did the Greek people like to see in their plays? _____

_____

How did the plays usually end? _____

_____

4. When were plays usually given in Greece?_____

_____

How many plays were given in a row? _____

5. How often were the Olympic Games held? _____

_____

In whose honor were the games held? _____

6. In what year were the first Olympic Games held? _____

How often are Olympic Games held now?_____

_____

II. **Circle True or False.**

T **F** 1. Dramas or plays were given in theaters.

T **F** 2. Hundreds of plays from ancient Greece still exist today.

51

T F 3. The Greeks liked plays about their gods and their rulers.

T F 4. Greek plays usually ended happily.

T F 5. The actors in Greek plays wore masks.

T F 6. Greek plays had much action and blood and violence.

T F 7. The Olympic Games were held every six years.

T F 8. The first Olympic Games were held in 776 B.C.

III. **Use the vocabulary words from the beginning of this chapter to complete each sentence below.**

1. Men and women who compete in games are called _____ .

2. Force which is used to injure or damage is called _____ .

3. Something that amuses or holds a person's interest is said to

_____ .

4. A play to be performed in a theater is known as a _____ .

5. When a person has to take the blame for what he does, we say he

is _____ for his actions.

IV. **Think about and discuss in class.**
In your dictionary find the two words below. Write their definitions.

tragedy: _____

_____

_____

comedy: _____

_____

_____

All over the world these masks stand for theater or drama. Why would masks be used to mean theater? _____

_____

Why are there *two* masks with different mouths? _____

_____

Have you ever been to a theater to see a play with live actors? _____

Did they wear masks? _____

Was the play a comedy or a tragedy? _____

_____

Tell your classmates about any plays you might have seen — even on television. _____

_____

North of Greece, Macedonia was becoming a powerful kingdom. Philip, Macedonia's king, wanted to unite the Greek city-states under his rule.

Philip admired Greek culture. He also wanted his son Alexander to be a good leader. He sent him to study with the great Greek philosopher Aristotle.

10 Getting Ready For Chapter Ten

Here are three vocabulary words that are used in the story of Philip of Macedonia. Use your dictionary and write a good definition of each to show that you understand the meaning.

1. tactics: _____

_____

2. respect: _____

_____

3. successor: _____

_____

I.

Answer these to help with your reading.

1. How did the other city-states feel about Athens? _____

_____

2. How did the wars between the city-states affect the Greeks? _____

_____

3. What country was to the north of Greece? _____

4. What did Philip want to do? _____

_____

Why was he not quick to make war on the Greeks? _____

_____

5. How did Philip organize the Greek city-states? _____

_____

6. Who did Philip then prepare to attack? _____

_____

What stopped him from doing this? _____

_____

7. Who was Philip's successor? _____

Who had been the new king's teacher? _____

How old was the new king when he began to rule? _____

II.

Circle the right word or words to complete the sentences below.

1. One Greek city-state was

   a. Greece   b. Athens   c. Persia

2. The country north of Greece was called

   a. Macedonia   b. Athens   c. California

3. Philip was Alexander's

    a. father   b. son   c. cousin

4. Philip prepared to attack

    a. Macedonia   b. Cuba   c. Persia

5. When Philip died, Alexander was

    a. ten years old   b. twenty years old   c. thirty years old

III. **Use one of the three vocabulary words from the beginning of this chapter to complete each sentence below.**

1. A person we show honor to is one we _____ .

2. The skill of arranging troops in battle is called _____ .

3. A person who becomes ruler after a parent has died is called the

    parent's _____ .

IV. **Think about and discuss in class.**

Philip had trained his son, Alexander, to be his successor. Because of this Alexander quickly became a strong king. But down through the ages, few rulers ever trained a successor. Often when rulers died their kingdoms or empires were lost. What things did Philip do to train Alexander to be king?

_____

_____

What other things could Philip have done to help train Alexander? _____

_____

How could these things have helped Alexander? _____

_____

Why do you think many rulers did not train successors? _____

_____

Why could it be unsafe to be a ruler? _____

58

The tall lighthouse that marked the city of Alexandria, Egypt, was called the Pharos.

An Asian coin more than two thousand years old shows a portrait of Alexander. He opened up new trade throughout the lands he conquered.

11

Getting Ready For Chapter Eleven

Here are two vocabulary words that are used in the story of Alexander the Great. Use your dictionary and write a good definition of each to show that you understand the meaning.

1. destiny: _____

_____

2. throne: _____

_____

Although he lived only thirty-four years, Alexander built an empire that stretched from Macedonia to the edge of India, more than three thousand miles.

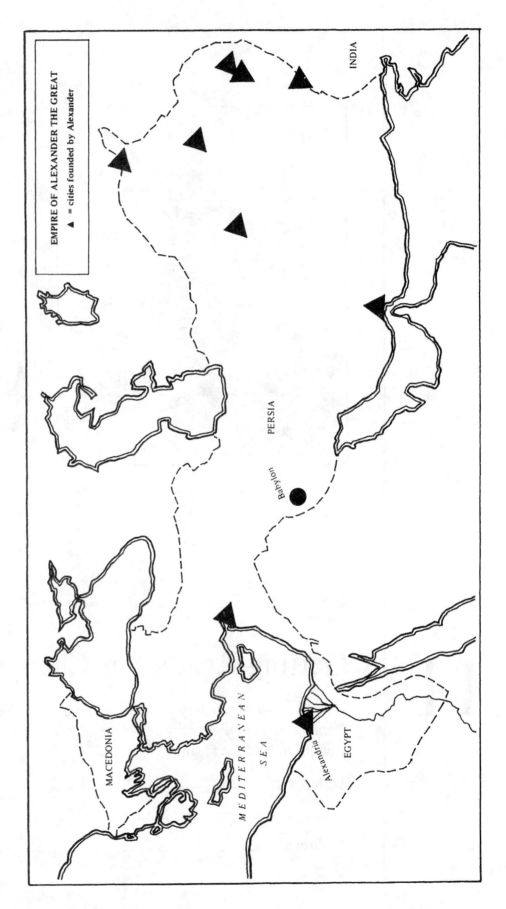

EMPIRE OF ALEXANDER THE GREAT

▲ = cities founded by Alexander

INDIA

PERSIA

Babylon

MACEDONIA

MEDITERRANEAN SEA

Alexandria

EGYPT

Chapter 11

Alexander the Great

Alexander was only twenty years old when he became king of Macedonia and all of Greece. He decided that he would carry out his father's plan to conquer Persia. Alexander loved the Greek civilization so much that he wanted to spread it everywhere. He believed that it was his **destiny** (DES-tuh-nee) to rule the world.

Three hundred years before the birth of Christ, Alexander ruled an army of thirty thousand soliders and five thousand horsemen. He turned his army to the east toward Persia. He did not know it, but Alexander would never return to Greece.

Alexander marched his army into Asia, winning battle after battle. Finally he fought (FAWT) the army of Darius III (duh-RY-us, the third), ruler of Persia. Darius had three times as many soldiers as Alexander. But Alexander's army fought bravely and won the battle. Darius was forced to run.

Alexander then marched his army to the old land of Egypt. He conquered Egypt and built a great city which he named for himself, Alexandria. Then he marched back to Persia to once more fight Darius. Again Alexander defeated him and again Darius ran. Later Darius was murdered by his own men. Alexander marched to the old city of Babylon and then to the capital city of Persia. Alexander took the **throne** (THROWN) of Persia. Greece was now completely safe from the Persians.

The next year, Alexander marched east to India, but his soliders grew tired. They forced him to turn back. Alexander set up his capital at Babylon. There he planned a world in which all people would live in peace. He wanted to spread the Greek civilization over all the known world. He planned many new cities.

Before Alexander could do all that he wanted, he died. Some historians think he died of a fever. Others think he was over-tired. He was only thirty-four years old at his death. After Alexander's death, his empire had no successor. It was divided into sections and three of his generals took control. Alexander had been a great leader of his army. He had also changed the whole Western world. He had spread Greek learning and ideas. He had opened new trade with the countries he conquered. He had earned the title, Alexander the Great.

I. Answer these to help with your reading.

1. What did the new king of Macedonia decide to do?_____

_____

What did he believe was his destiny? _____

_____

2. Toward what country did Alexander turn his large army? _____

_____

3. Whose army did Alexander fight in Persia? _____

_____

4. What city did Alexander build in the old land of Egypt?_____

_____

5. What country did Alexander conquer to make Greece safe? _____

_____

6. Why didn't Alexander's soldiers march into India? _____

_____

_____

What kind of world did Alexander plan while at Babylon?_____

_____

7. How do historians think Alexander died? _____

_____

How old was he at his death? _____

8. What happened to Alexander's empire after his death? _____

_____

_____

9. What did Alexander do to earn the title "the Great"?_____

_____

_____

II.   **Circle the right word or words to complete the sentences below.**

1. Alexander wanted to spread the Greek civilization

    a. to Macedonia   b. everywhere   c. to Persia

2. Alexander fought

    a. Darius I   b. Darius II   c. Darius III

3. Darius was the ruler of

    a. Persia   b. Egypt   c. Babylon

4. The army of Darius was

    a. smaller than   b. larger than Alexander's   c. the same size
       Alexander's   as Alexander's

5. Alexander defeated Darius and his army

    a. one time   b. two times   c. four times

6. After turning back from India, Alexander set up his capital at

    a. Egypt   b. Macedonia   c. Babylon

7. When Alexander died, control of the empire went to

    a. three of his generals   b. his mother   c. his father

III.   **Use one of the two vocabulary words from the beginning of this chapter to complete each sentence below.**

1. The chair on which a ruler sits during a ceremony is called the

    _____ .

2. What becomes of a person or is bound to happen to a person is that

    person's_____ .

IV.   **Think about and discuss in class.**

In ancient times, people built a tall lighthouse in the city of Alexandria, Egypt. This lighthouse was called "The Pharos" (FAIR-ohss). The Pharos was described as one of the Seven Wonders of the Ancient World.

Have you ever heard of the Seven Wonders of the World? _____

Choose one person to go to the library and get an encyclopedia that tells of the Seven Wonders of the Ancient World. (They may be listed in the "S" volume, or in the "W"—for "Wonders"—volume.) Many encyclopedias show pictures of them all.

Make a list of the Seven Wonders of the Ancient World.

1. _____

2. _____

3. _____

4. _____

5. _____

6. _____

7. _____

Only one of the Seven Wonders is still standing. Do you know which one?

_____

Which one of the Seven Wonders do you like best? _____

Are there any buildings in your city or that you have seen that might be

"wonders" of the modern world?_____

_____

_____

A Black general named Cleitus was in charge of Alexander's cavalry.

Alexander's Black General

When Alexander the Great left Greece to conquer the Persians, he took with him a Black general named Cleitus (KLY-tus). Cleitus was in charge of Alexander's horsemen. He was such a good general that he was made king of Bactria (BAK-tree-uh), a city in Asia.

In a great battle with Darius, the king of Persia, Cleitus saved the day by saving the life of Alexander. While Alexander was busy fighting two Persian generals with his sword, a third Persian came up behind Alexander with an axe. Alexander was struck once on the head. When the Persian raised his axe to kill, Cleitus ran him through the body with his spear.

Alexander and Cleitus did not always agree on everything. Cleitus believed that Alexander enjoyed rich living too much. He tried to change Alexander and this caused trouble between the two. One night when Alexander had been drinking, the two men began to fight. Their friends stopped the fight. But as Cleitus was leaving, Alexander threw a spear at him, hitting his heart. Alexander's good friend was dead. Upset by what he had done, Alexander tried to kill himself. His guards stopped him. For three days he refused to eat or drink. He called himself a murderer and said that he wanted to die. Alexander never forgave himself for the murder of his brave general.

The Etruscans, who built an early civilization in Italy, were skilled craftsmen and made jewelry, metal goods, and pottery to trade to other lands. Shown here are some Etruscan objects that archeologists have found: a gold pin to fasten a garment, a painting of a man holding a bronze dish, some pottery jugs, and a scene from the side of a decorated bowl.

Italy is a peninsula shaped like a
high-heeled boot. At its top are
the mountains known as the
Alps, and near its "toe" is the
island of Sicily.

12 Getting Ready For Chapter Twelve

Here are three vocabulary words that are used in the story of Italy and its early
people. Use your dictionary and write a good definition of each to show that
you understand the meaning.

1. colonist: _____

_____

2. peninsula: _____

_____

3. Europe: _____

_____

Chapter 12   Italy and Its Early People

We have been reading about civilizations that were all near the Mediterranean Sea. The Egyptians, the Babylonians, the Phoenicians, the Hebrews and the Minoans all traded their goods and ideas. They spread civilization over the lands on the eastern shores of the Mediterranean. Then the Greeks built upon these civilizations by adding their ideas. In doing so, they helped people progress even more. Alexander the Great and Greek **colonists** (KOL-u-nusts) spread Greek ideas and civilization far and wide. Some Greek colonies were begun on the western shores of the Mediterranean.

Most of the people who lived around the western shores of the Mediterranean Sea became civilized much later than those around its eastern shores. At first these people were small farmers. They learned from more civilized neighbors (NAY-burs). They also learned to make war and conquered the older civilizations. Then they built a civilization of their own.

Near the middle of the Mediterranean Sea is a long, narrow **peninsula** (puh-NIN-suh-luh). This **peninsula** is called Italy. It is shaped like a boot. Near the toe of the boot is a large island called Sicily (SIS-uh-lee). Greece had many colonies on Sicily as well as in the south of Italy. The Greek **colonists** brought their civilization with them to Sicily and southern Italy.

To the north of Italy are very high mountains, the Alps. The Alps cut Italy off from the rest of **Europe** (YUR-up). The eastern side of Italy is mountainous. But the western side is a flat plain. Here farming is good. Because there were plains instead of steep mountains and narrow valleys as in Greece, it was easier to unite the people of Italy into a single country.

The northern plain of Italy was the home of a group of people called Etruscans (ee-TRUSS-kuns). In many ways, the Etruscans were like the Minoans. They learned to write their own language. They used Greek letters that they had learned from the Greek **colonists** who lived to the south and on Sicily. Like the Minoans, Etruscans built cities and towns and made goods to trade with others. They were known for their beautiful pottery and gold and silver jewelry. The Etruscans were the most civilized people in Italy except for the Greek **colonists**.

I.

Answer these to help with your reading.

1. Where were all the civilizations located that we have been reading about?

_____

_____

2. What peoples spread civilization over the lands on the *eastern* shores of the Mediterranean Sea? _____

_____

3. At first what kind of work was done by the people who lived on the *western* shores of the Mediterranean Sea? _____

_____

4. What is the name of the peninsula near the middle of the Mediterranean Sea? _____

_____

What is the large island near Italy called? _____

5. Where are the Alps? _____

_____

6. Why was it easier to unite the people of Italy into a single country than it was to unite the Greeks? _____

_____

7. Who were the most civilized people in Italy except for the Greek colonists?

_____

Where was their home? _____

_____

II.

Circle True or False.

T   F   1. Greek colonists helped to spread Greek ideas and civilization far and wide.

T F 2. The people on the western shores of the Mediterranean became civilized before those around its eastern shores.

T F 3. The farmers on the eastern shores of the Mediterranean later built a great civilization of their own.

T F 4. Italy is shaped like a football.

T F 5. The Alps cut Italy off from the rest of Europe.

T F 6. The western part of Europe is a flat plain.

T F 7. The Etruscans were not civilized.

T F 8. The Etruscans were like the Minoans in many ways.

III. **Use one of the three vocabulary words from the beginning of this chapter to complete each of the sentences below.**

1. Italy is part of the continent called _____ .

2. A person who is sent by his own country to live on and farm in another country is called a _____ .

3. A long narrow piece of land that is surrounded by water on three sides is called a _____ .

A Review of Vocabulary Words

On the lines, write the correct vocabulary word from the bottom of the page to show that you can say each word. Then match the words in Column A with the correct definitions in Column B. Draw lines to the right definitions. When everyone is finished, discuss the words and their meanings to be sure each person has them right.

Column A	Column B
(fuh-LOSS-uh-fee) _____ •	• a high hill above a city
(EM-pyr) _____ •	• ways to use an army
(ree-SPEKT) _____ •	• a play given in a theater
(DRAHM-uh) _____ •	• sworn as the truth
(LEV-er) _____ •	• a tool used to pry
(OHTH) _____ •	• all lands under one ruler
(uh-KROP-uh-liss) _____ •	• the study of life and the love of wisdom
(puh-NIN-suh-luh) _____ •	• next in line to be ruler
(ATH-leet) _____ •	• a narrow piece of land surrounded on three sides by water
(DES-tuh-nee) _____ •	• what one is born to do
(TAK-tiks) _____ •	• to show honor to
(suk-SESS-ur) _____ •	• a man or woman who competes in games

empire	tactics	oath	athlete
respect	philosophy	drama	Acropolis
lever	peninsula	destiny	successor

Romulus and Remus were twin
brothers adopted by a she-wolf.
The Romans believed that
Romulus founded the city of
Rome.

13 Getting Ready For Chapter Thirteen

Here are four vocabulary words that are used in the story of the founding of
Rome. Use your dictionary and write a good definition of each to show that
you understand the meaning.

1. site: _____

_____

2. cruel: _____

_____

3. citizen: _____

_____

4. senate: _____

_____

Chapter 13

The Founding of Rome

Halfway down the peninsula of Italy, the Tiber (TY-bur) River flows west to the sea. South of this river lived several tribes of farmers and shepherds. They were called Latins. To the north of the Tiber River lived the Etruscans. The Etruscans often came to the Tiber to trade pottery, jewelry and other goods with the Latins. A trading post grew on one of seven hills by the river. Then a town grew which covered all seven hills. The town was named Rome.

Historians are not sure when the town of Rome was started or founded. The Romans thought that the city of Rome was founded in the year 753 B.C. The Romans, like the Greeks before them, made up stories to explain things. They had a story to explain the founding of the city of Rome.

The Romans tell of twin brothers named Romulus and Remus (ROM-yoo-lus and REE-mus). Their mother was human and their father was a god. While the twins were still tiny babies, they were placed in a basket and put into the Tiber River. The basket sailed down the river until it floated to shore. A she-wolf found the babies and fed and cared for them. When they grew up, they decided to found a great city. They fought over where the city was to be built. In the fight Romulus killed Remus. He then chose a **site** (SYT) for his city. He named the city Rome after himself. The Romans loved the story of Romulus and Remus. They told it often.

About 600 B.C., when Rome was still a small place, Etruscan rulers took control of the town. They made Rome into a city of many buildings. They built great sewers to drain the land. They taught (TAWT) the people of Rome new ways to build. The Etruscan rulers set up the first Roman government. They chose people of high rank to be members of the **Senate** (SEN-ut). The **Senate** helped the leader rule.

The Etruscans ruled Rome for about a hundred years. After a time the Etruscan rulers became mean and **cruel** (KROO-ul). Finally, the Romans turned against their Etruscan king and drove him out of Rome. Then the **citizens** (SIT-uh-zuns) set up a government of elected officers. The male **citizens** met once a year to choose the officers. It was a high honor in Rome to be a government officer. The **Senate** continued to help the officers do their jobs. Senators were not elected by the people, but were chosen by the heads of the government.

After Rome had freed itself from the rule of the Etruscan leaders, Greek colonists to the south began to sail their boats up the Tiber River. They came

Greek colonists living to the south of Rome sailed up the Tiber River to trade their goods with the Roman people.

Important Roman men were members of the Senate. In early times, they advised the rulers. In later times, the Senate came to hold most of the real power in Rome.

to trade Greek goods with the Roman people. The Greek traders taught the Romans how to build ships. The Romans also learned how to use the Greek alphabet for their own writing. The Romans learned and copied much of the civilization of the Greeks.

The Romans did not copy the Greek form of government. The early Romans would never have put up with the kind of fighting that went on between the Greek city-states. They believed in one strong government which worked for the good of all **citizens**. Eventually the Roman people would build and rule a very large empire that would last for hundreds of years. The Greeks had never been able to do this.

I.

Answer these to help with your reading.

1. What river flows to the sea in Italy? _____

   What tribes lived south of the river? _____

   _____

   What people lived to the north? _____

   _____

2. How many hills did the town of Rome cover? _____

3. Who found the twin babies, Romulus and Remus, and fed and cared for them? _____

   _____

   Which brother founded the city of Rome? _____

4. Who made Rome into a big city? _____

   _____

5. Why did the Romans turn against the Etruscan leader? _____

   _____

6. How often did the male citizens of Rome choose their officers? _____

_____

What group helped the leader? _____

7. Who taught the Romans how to build ships? _____

_____

II.   **Circle the right word or words to complete each sentence below.**

1. The Tiber River flows

    a. east to the sea   b. north to the sea   c. west to the sea

2. The tribes of farmers south of the Tiber were called

    a. Africans   b. Greeks   c. Latins

3. The Roman story said that in 753 B.C.

    a. Greece was founded   b. Rome was founded   c. Macedonia was founded

4. Romulus and Remus were

    a. sisters   b. twin brothers   c. cousins

5. The Romans said that the founder of Rome was

    a. Romulus   b. Remus   c. Alexander

6. The Romans turned against the cruel rule of the

    a. Babylonians   b. Etruscans   c. Greeks

7. In Rome the government was run by the

    a. male citizens   b. Greeks   c. Latins

8. Senators were chosen by

    a. Romulus   b. the people   c. the heads of government

III. **Use one of the four vocabulary words from the beginning of this chapter to complete each of the sentences below.**

1. A person who goes out of his way to be unkind to people and animals

   is _____ .

2. A place where something is located is a _____ .

3. When someone is born in a country, he becomes a _____ of that country.

4. A body of governing lawmakers can be called a _____ .

IV. **Think about and discuss in class.**

Italy and Greece are part of a continent named Europe. The old kingdoms of Phoenicia, Babylonia, and Israel were part of the continent of Asia. The land of Egypt is on the continent of Africa. What is a continent? Look for the word in your dictionary and write the meaning below.

_____

_____

_____

_____

_____

The earth has seven continents. Use a world map to name all seven.

1. _____

2. _____

3. _____

4. _____

5. _____

6. _____

7. _____

Much of the planet earth is covered with salt water. This water is found in oceans. The earth has four large oceans. Using a world map, see if you can name all four. (Your teacher can help you.)

1. _____

2. _____

3. _____

4. _____

Smaller oceans on the earth are called seas. Can you write the name of the sea

that all the civilizations you have read about are near?_____

_____

After about a hundred years of fighting, the Roman army finally destroyed the city of Carthage.

After they defeated Carthage, the Romans had the most powerful navy of any land in the ancient world. Their ships sailed all over the Mediterranean Sea. Some historians say the Mediterranean was like a Roman lake.

14 Getting Ready For Chapter Fourteen

Here are two vocabulary words that are used in the story of the wars with Carthage. Use your dictionary and write a good definition of each to show that you understand the meaning.

1. ally: _____

_____

2. revenge: _____

_____

The people of Rome and Carthage fought many sea battles to decide who would control trade routes and the island of Sicily.

In the middle of winter Hannibal, a great general from Carthage, led his army across the Alps to make a surprise attack on the Romans. Elephants that he had brought with him from Africa carried his supplies.

Chapter 14

The Wars with Carthage

As Rome grew, the Romans were able to conquer all the people of Italy. They even conquered the Greek colonists who lived to the south. Soon all the peoples of the peninsula had come under Roman control. By letting these peoples rule themselves, the Romans made strong **allies** (AL-ize). Each **ally** had to promise never to make war on Rome. They also agreed to let Rome use their armies at any time.

Across the Mediterranean on the coast of Africa was a great city named Carthage (KAR-thij). Carthage had been a trading colony of old Phoenicia. It was a very wealthy city with many ships. Carthage controlled all the trade of the western Mediterranean.

As Rome grew, Roman ships sailed farther and farther to trade. Carthage became afraid that Rome would take over her trade and her colonies. Carthage and Rome finally went to war over control of trade and the control of Sicily. The Romans had to build many ships to fight this sea war. The war with Carthage went on for one hundred years. Historians call these wars the Punic (PYOO-nik) Wars. "Punic" was the Phoenician word for the language spoken in Carthage.

Finally, the Romans were able to defeat the navy of Carthage and take control of Sicily. Carthage gave up Sicily but soon tried to conquer all of Spain. The Romans had colonies in Spain and did not like this. The war began again.

This time Carthage had a young Black general leading its army. His name was Hannibal (HAN-u-bul). He was one of the greatest generals in all history. Even the Romans, who hated and feared Hannibal, had admiration for him.

Hannibal decided to settle the contest between Rome and Carthage. He planned to lead his army into Italy and fight until Rome was defeated. The only way to reach Rome by land was to cross the Alps and then to march south. The Alps are very high and very rugged and cold. The Romans believed it was impossible for anyone to cross the Alps with an army. Hannibal knew he would surprise the Romans and defeat them if he crossed the Alps.

In Spain, Hannibal built a large army. He had many soldiers and horsemen as well as thirty-seven elephants which he brought with him from Africa. Hannibal marched his army out of Spain and over the Alps into Italy. Historians wonder how he was ever able to do this, for Hannibal crossed the Alps in winter. He lost many men on the long march.

When the Romans learned that Hannibal and his army had crossed the Alps, they were frightened because he was so close. Then they heard how tired and small his army was. They rushed to attack with a huge army. But Hannibal had decided already what tactics he would use. He had his men in good positions. He backed them up with his elephants and his swordsmen. It was not long before he had the Romans running back to Rome.

Hannibal spent many years in Italy, winning battle after battle against the Roman armies. But he never conquered the city of Rome itself. Finally, the Romans sent an army to attack Carthage. Hannibal was called back to Carthage to protect his own city.

The Romans defeated Hannibal and destroyed the city of Carthage. The Romans wanted to kill Hannibal but he escaped. They followed him to Athens and then into Asia. When Hannibal was trapped in an Asian city, he cheated the Romans of their **revenge** (ree-VENJ). He carried poison in a secret compartment of his ring. He swallowed the poison and died.

The wars with Carthage made Rome a great power in the Mediterranean. Now Rome had a large army and a great navy. The Roman navy sailed east on the Mediterranean. They conquered Greece and Macedonia. They took Asia Minor, Syria and even Egypt. Some historians say that the Mediterranean became a Roman lake because Rome ruled all its shores. Rome became the most important city in the ancient world.

I. **Answer these to help with your reading.**
1. How did the Romans make strong allies? _____

_____

What did the allies have to promise? _____

_____

2. What great city was on the coast of Africa? _____

What people had started this city as a trading colony? _____

3. Why did Carthage and Rome go to war? _____

_____

How long did these wars last? _____

What were these wars called? _____

4. What was the name of the young Black general of Carthage? _____

How did he march into Italy? _____

5. How did the Romans finally get Hannibal out of their country? _____

_____

6. After the defeat of Carthage, where did the Roman navy sail? _____

_____

What countries did they conquer? _____

_____

7. What city became most important at this time in the ancient world? _____

_____

II.   **Draw lines to match each word in List A with the right definition in List B.**

List A	List B
Hannibal ●	● city on African coast
Punic Wars ●	● most important city in ancient world
ancient Rome ●	● island south of Italy
Carthage ●	● between Rome and Carthage
Alps ●	● the great general of Carthage
Sicily ●	● mountains north of Italy

III. **Use one of the two vocabulary words from the beginning of this chapter to complete each of the sentences below.**

1. To do harm in return for harm done to you is to take _____ .

2. Any country that is the friend of another country so that both countries will

   be safe from enemies is an _____ .

IV. **Think about and discuss in class.**

Hannibal was one of the world's greatest generals. He knew that the best way to fight the Romans would be to attack Italy and then Rome. He also knew the safest way to enter Italy was from the north. The Romans would never expect an army to come over the Alps.

Why do you think Hannibal took elephants to Italy? _____

_____

How do you think he lost many men crossing the Alps? _____

_____

Once Hannibal was in Italy, where do you think his army got food? _____

_____

The Romans could not defeat Hannibal in Italy. They decided to attack the city of Carthage. When Carthage was in danger, Hannibal was called to help. Hannibal had to leave Italy. Carthage was a powerful city with high walls. It was not easy for the Romans to conquer it.

How do you think the Romans would attack such a city? _____

_____

What kinds of weapons would they use? _____

_____

Roman law stated that some of the emperors were gods. People of the empire had to worship before statues of these emperors.

The market place and meeting place in Rome was called the Forum. Around it were the banks and businesses and government buildings.

15

Getting Ready For Chapter Fifteen

Here are four vocabulary words that are used in the story about life in Rome. Use your dictionary and write a good definition of each to show that you understand the meaning.

1. aqueduct: _____

_____

2. forum: _____

_____

3. republic: _____

_____

4. veto: _____

_____

The Romans built aqueducts to bring water from lakes to their homes and other buildings.

Chapter 15

Life in Rome

The Romans built fine roads for their armies. These roads also made moving goods easier and helped trade. The roads entered Rome from every direction. It was said at the time that all roads led to Rome. The Romans built large **aqueducts** (AK-wuh-dukts) to bring fresh water into their city.

Like Athens, Rome had its marketplace and meeting place. It was called the Roman **forum** (FOR-um). The **forum** was crowded with people every day. Buildings of the government, the Senate and the law courts (KORTS) were part of the **forum**. Banks and businesses were nearby.

The government of Rome was called a **republic** (ree-PUB-lik). This was because there was no single ruler, no king. The leaders of Rome were chosen by the people. In addition to these elected leaders there was a group of important men who made up the Senate.

A few old and very rich families of Rome owned most of the land. The members of these families were called patricians (puh-TRISH-uns). At first, only patricians were allowed to be members of the Senate. The poor people were called plebeians (pleh-BEE-uns). Plebeians had little power in the government. Later they won some rights and could send officers to the Senate. The officers who represented the plebeians were called tribunes (TRIB-yoons). Their job was to help protect the rights of the common people.

The plebeians made the Senate write down the laws of Rome for all to see. This way everyone could know the laws. The written laws were placed in the **forum** where anyone could read them. As time passed, many plebeians became rich businessmen of Rome. Then they were allowed to be members of the Senate.

As the Roman army conquered more lands the generals brought slaves to Rome. The slaves did the hard work around the house and on the farms. Often the slaves were Greek and had the extra job of helping teach Roman children. Young Roman boys of families that could afford slaves were trained to be good citizens of Rome. They learned to read and to write and were taught Greek ideas and the Roman ways of government. The girls were trained by their mothers to keep the house. The women were in charge of the household slaves. Roman houses were small at first but as Rome grew richer, the houses grew larger and the women's responsibilities grew.

The Romans had many gods. Most of their gods were the same as the Greek gods but the Romans gave them different names. Zeus became Jupiter (JOO-pit-er). Ares (AIR-eez) became Mars, and Hermes (HER-meez) became Mercury (MER-ku-ree). The Romans had altars in their homes. The women and girls were in charge of the household altars. Romans could worship their gods often.

As the Roman armies conquered more lands, they brought home treasure. Rome became a wealthy city. More and more people became rich. Fewer Roman citizens were needed to do the hard work. Slaves, who became very cheap to buy, were used for that. There was more food in Rome than was needed. Many Roman farmers sold their land and moved into the city. Instead of many small farms, there came to be a few huge farms owned by the rich and worked by slaves. Rome grew into a crowded city. Large numbers of the people in Rome had little to do each day, and the Romans developed some special ways for these idle men and women to pass their days away.

I. **Answer these to help with your reading.**
1. According to an old saying, where did all roads lead? _____

   What use does an aqueduct have? _____

   _____

2. In Rome, what was the marketplace called? _____

   What buildings were there? _____

   _____

3. What was the government of Rome called? _____

4. What were the rich people of Rome called? _____

   What were the poor people called? _____

5. Whose job was it to help protect the rights of the common people? _____

   _____

6. What did the Roman generals bring to Rome? _____

   _____

7. Where did many Roman farmers move? _____

II.

Circle True or False.

T   F   1. The plebeians sent tribunes to the Senate.

T   F   2. The plebeians made the Senate write the laws of Rome for all to see.

T   F   3. The Roman gods had the same names as the Greek gods.

T   F   4. The Romans had very little food to eat.

T   F   5. The price of a slave was always very high.

III.

Use one of the four vocabulary words from the beginning of this chapter to complete each of the sentences below.

1. The meeting and marketplace of an ancient Roman city was the

   _____ .

2. The power or right to forbid or prevent something is the power of

   _____ .

3. A nation or state without a single ruler and where citizens choose the

   government officials is called a _____ .

4. A big trough that carries water from one place to another is called

   an _____ .

IV.

Think about and discuss in class.

In many ways, life in Rome was like life in any large city today. What

roads lead to your city? _____

_____

How does your city get fresh water? _____

Is there any place in your city like the Roman forum? _____

How is it different from the forum? _____

_____

Romans enjoyed watching chariot races. These were held in a large circular stadium called the Circus Maximus. Drivers of the chariots often died because of the sharp turns in the track that made collisions happen easily.

To honor a winning general, Rome would hold a celebration called a Triumph. There was always a parade to show off prisoners his army had captured.

Gladiators fought each other, often to the death, before crowds of Roman people. The gladiators were usually slaves or prisoners of war.

16 Getting Ready For Chapter Sixteen

Here are four vocabulary words that are used in the story of Roman entertainment. Use your dictionary and write a good definition of each to show that you understand the meaning.

1. distant: _____

_____

2. gladiator: _____

_____

3. shield: _____

_____

4. captive: _____

_____

Chapter 16 Roman Entertainment

The ancient city of Rome grew very large and crowded. Many of the people living there did not have to work. The government gave them food and a bit of money. The government also put on shows for all the people. The price of a ticket was very low.

A favorite show of the Romans was chariot racing. In Rome, the chariot races were held at the Circus Maximus (SUR-kus MAX-i-mus), or the "Great Ring." There were races every day. The race track was a half mile around and a race was seven times around the track. The turns were very sharp and there were many smashups.

Each chariot was pulled by four horses. The drivers were very daring and many were killed. Those who were lucky and won races often became rich. The prize for the winner was money. Homing pigeons (PIJ-uns) were sent with the names of winners to **distant** (DIS-tunt) cities. The chariot races were very popular all over the Roman lands.

Another entertainment that the people loved was a **gladiator** (GLAD-ee-ay-tur) fight. Such fights were held in a large building called the Colosseum (kol-u-SEE-um). The Colosseum was like a football stadium (STAYD-ee-um). It had a canvas (KAN-vuss) roof. Most **gladiators** were prisoners of war or slaves. They had been trained to fight. Some were promised their freedom if they could win a certain number of fights. A few won their freedom and even became citizens of Rome. **Gladiators** were armed with swords and **shields** (SHEELDS). They fought until one was wounded. Then the crowd decided if the wounded **gladiator** should be killed. Some historians say "thumbs up" meant he was a good fighter and should live. "Thumbs down" meant he must die. The crowd usually liked to see blood. Many **gladiators** died in fights at the Colosseum.

Sometimes whole armies of **gladiators** would fight battles in the Colosseum. They even had to fight lions and tigers. Once ten thousand **gladiators** were killed in one month. These fights were held for many years in Rome.

The men of Rome had another pastime. The city had over nine hundred public baths. It cost less than one penny to enter a bath. Any man could afford that because the government gave each man some money. Most baths were very large buildings built by the government. They had heated swimming pools and steam rooms. The baths were heated by fires in the basement. The fires were kept burning by slaves.

Many Roman men went to the baths every day. They usually went after lunch and stayed all afternoon. They played games and did exercises. They swam and met friends to talk. Some baths even had libraries and reading rooms for the men to use.

Another kind of entertainment took place when a Roman general brought his army back to Rome after winning battles. A big celebration would be held for him. This celebration was called a Triumph (TRY-umf). It was a great honor. There was always a parade. First came government officers and senators. Then came wagons full of gold and silver that had been taken in the battles. These were followed by **captives** (KAP-tivs) who would become slaves. The parade went to the forum. Then there was a feast. Later the army would put on a show and kill many **captives**. Sometimes a Roman Triumph lasted for many days. The generals became very popular with the people because of these celebrations.

I. **Answer these to help with your reading.**

1. Who gave the people of Rome food and a bit of money? _____

_____

What entertainment was put on for the people? _____

_____

2. What show was held at the Circus Maximus? _____

_____

How were the names of winners sent to distant cities? _____

_____

3. What shows were held in the Colosseum? _____

_____

What did "thumbs-up" mean? _____

_____

What did "thumbs-down" mean? _____

_____

4. Tell some things Roman men did at the baths. _____

_____

_____

_____

5. What did the Romans call the party given a Roman general and his army?

_____

How did they celebrate? _____

_____

_____

_____

_____

II. **Circle the right word or words to complete the sentences below.**
1. The Circus Maximus had

    a. a railroad   b. a race track   c. no events

2. Roman racing chariots were pulled by

    a. one horse   b. three horses   c. four horses

3. The Colosseum was like a

    a. forum   b. square   c. football stadium

4. During a Triumph the army killed many

    a. captives   b. Romans   c. senators

III. **Use one of the four vocabulary words from the beginning of this chapter to complete each of the following sentences.**
1. Something that is far away is _____ .

2. A piece of armor used for protection in battle is a _____ .

3. Men who fought in the Roman Colosseum were called _____ .

4. A prisoner of war is a _____ .

IV.

Think about and discuss in class.
The Romans liked to be entertained. Many times their entertainment was violent and cruel. What entertainment do we have today that is violent or cruel? _____

What shows are most popular on TV? _____

_____

_____

What movies are most popular? _____

_____

How many of the TV shows and movies you listed show much violence and cruelty? _____

_____

If you have ever seen an auto race, what is your favorite part of the race?_____

_____

If you have ever seen a boxing or wrestling match or the roller derby, what do you enjoy most about them?_____

_____

_____

Do you think there is too much violence in today's entertainment?_____

_____

What effect do you think seeing violence has on you and your neighbors?_____

_____

_____

Julius Caesar was Rome's greatest general. When he became leader of Rome, the old republic came to an end and a time of one-man rule began. Caesar called himself "emperor" because the word "king" was hated by the Romans.

Octavian was the adopted son of Julius Caesar and became the next emperor of Rome. As emperor, he changed his name to Augustus.

AVGVSTVS

Augustus made the Roman lands into a strong, united empire that covered parts of Europe, the Middle East, and Africa. Under Roman government, this part of the world stayed peaceful for two hundred years.

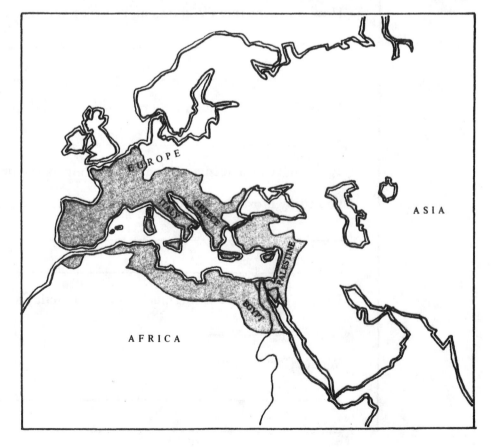

Julius Caesar did not live to carry out all his plans for improving the Roman government. About four years after he became leader of Rome, he was assassinated by his enemies.

17

Getting Ready For Chapter Seventeen

Here are four vocabulary words that are used in the story of the end of the Roman Republic. Use your dictionary and write a good definition of each to show that you understand the meaning.

1. politician: _____

_____

2. governor: _____

_____

3. province: _____

_____

4. dictator: _____

_____

Chapter 17   The End of the Republic

Although Rome was becoming richer, its government was becoming less and less fair. Over the years, the Senate gained more and more power. It favored the rich and noble families and was unwilling to pass laws that would help the common people. It would not give people in the Roman provinces the right to vote. In addition, many senators were dishonest.

From time to time, a few **politicians** (pol-uh-TISH-uns) would try to improve things. One of these politicians was Julius Caesar (JOOL-yus SEE-zer). Caesar served in the government for a while and won the trust of the common people. Then he served as **governor** (GUV-er-ner) of a province, conquering many tribes and winning new land for Rome. He became Rome's greatest general. Historians say he was as great as Hannibal or Alexander. Caesar built up a large army that loved him and would follow him loyally.

Caesar believed he could do much good as leader of the country. He made himself **dictator** (DIK-tayt-er) for life. By making himself the only ruler, he brought an end to the Roman republic. A republic is a country ruled by many people together, but a dictatorship is a country ruled by one person alone. Knowing that Romans hated the memory of their early kings, Caesar did not call himself "king." He used a new title — **"emperor"** (EM-per-er).

Caesar tried to change the government in Rome and in the **provinces** to one that was honest. He tried to help the poor people. He was known as a wise and fair ruler. But Caesar did not live to complete his work. His enemies in the Senate murdered him. They stabbed Caesar to death.

Caesar had named his adopted son, Octavian (ok-TAY-vee-un), to be his successor. Octavian was only nineteen years old when Caesar died but he was very wise. He took control of Caesar's old army and made war against the men who had killed Caesar. Finally, he defeated them.

When he became emperor, Octavian changed his name to Augustus (aw-GUS-tus). His rule began a time of strong rule for Rome. For two hundred years this strong rule would give Rome peace. Never since then have so many people lived without a war for so long a time. Augustus made the Roman lands into a strong empire. There were millions of people in the empire. They were of many races. All were protected by the Roman army. All paid taxes to Rome. All lived under strong Roman law.

Augustus ruled for many years. He made Rome a greater city by replacing old buildings with new ones made of marble. He brought good government to Rome and the whole Roman Empire.

After Augustus died, there were many more emperors of Rome. A few were very good rulers and worked for the good of Rome. Most were very bad and cared nothing about the people. But they did keep the empire strong.

I.

Answer these to help with your reading.

1. As Rome became rich and powerful, what happened to its government?

_____

2. What politician won the trust of the common people?_____

3. What title did Julius Caesar give to himself? _____

How did Caesar die? _____

_____

4. Who was Caesar's successor? _____

To what did he change his name? _____

For how many years did Rome have peace? _____

5. Tell three things *all* people in the Roman Empire shared. _____

_____

_____

II.

Circle the right word or words to complete each sentence below.

1. The Senate favored

   a. the common people   b. Julius Caesar   c. noble families

2. Caesar was Rome's greatest

   a. general   b. senator   c. historian

3. Julius Caesar was governor of a Roman

   a. temple   b. emperor   c. province

4. When Caesar took control of all Rome, he called himself

    a. emperor   b. senator   c. general

5. Caesar made himself a

    a. successor   b. dictator for life   c. citizen

6. Caesar's successor changed his name to

    a. Octavian   b. Alexander   c. Augustus

III.   **Use one of the four vocabulary words from the beginning of this chapter to complete each of the sentences below.**

1. One-person rule is carried out by a _____ .

2. A person who controls or manages the people of a certain area or a province

    is a _____ .

3. A person who understands the ways of government and works in it is

    a _____ .

4. An area of land and its peoples brought under the control of the Roman

    government was called a _____ .

IV.   **Think about and discuss in class.**

Julius Caesar and his successor, Augustus, made changes in the calendar. They made the calendar that we use today. Two of the months are named after them.

What month do you think is named for Julius Caesar?_____

What month is named for Augustus? _____

Which month was named for the Roman god Mars? _____

The Romans had a god named Janus. This god had a face on both sides of his

head. What month was named for Janus? _____

Why would the name of the god with two faces be used for this month? _____

_____

When Octavian's army conquered Egypt, Cleopatra killed herself. Legends say that she chose a poisonous snake as her means of death.

A Fascinating Queen of Egypt

While Julius Caesar was rising to power in Rome, a young, determined woman became the queen of Egypt. Her name was Cleopatra (klee-uh-PAT-ruh). Dramatists and movie-makers have been fascinated by her story.

Cleopatra was only eighteen when she began to rule, but she was intelligent and brave. As queen, she had two main aims: to make her own situation strong and secure, and to win a share of power in the Roman world around her. She succeeded in doing both of these things because of her influence over two Roman leaders, Caesar and Mark Antony.

She got the chance to make a friend of Caesar when he was near Egypt, fighting enemies of Rome. Cleopatra thought that if she helped Caesar, he might help her. Caesar did use his army to strengthen Cleopatra's control of her kingdom — he also fell in love with her and took her with him to Rome. Caesar and Cleopatra may have thought about uniting their lands to make one vast empire. But before they could carry out such a plan, Caesar was killed. Cleopatra returned to Egypt.

Caesar's death led to a power struggle in Rome. At first, Octavian had to share the empire with a popular politician named Mark Antony. Antony took charge of the territories in the east, and there he had a meeting with Cleopatra. She charmed him and gave him expensive gifts. Antony married her and stayed with her in Egypt, planning a huge eastern kingdom that Cleopatra and he could rule. But back in Italy, Octavian stirred up the Romans against Mark Antony and the foreign queen.

Cleopatra wisely sensed that war would come. She urged her husband to prepare for battle and helped him with troops and supplies. She knew that if Octavian defeated them, her kingdom would be swallowed up by Rome.

Octavian did win the war. As he marched into Egypt with his army, Cleopatra and Antony decided to end their lives. They could not bear the thought of being taken to prison in Rome. It is possible that Cleopatra chose to die from a snakebite. She might have done this because a snake stood for the kingdom of Egypt, which her family had ruled for almost 300 years. At any rate, Egypt did become a Roman province, but Octavian had no royal prisoners to take home for his Triumphal parade. A large picture of Cleopatra was all he could show off to the crowds in the streets of Rome.

Germans who lived north of
Rome invaded in A.D. 410 and
burned many of the buildings. In
476 a German became the ruler
of Rome.

18

Getting Ready For Chapter Eighteen

Here are two vocabulary words that are used in the story of Christianity and
the fall of Rome. Use your dictionary and write a good definition of each to
show that you understand the meaning.

1. Christian: _____

_____

2. disappear: _____

_____

The eastern part of the Roman Empire lasted for a thousand years. Its capital city was Constantinople, built at the place where Europe and Asia come together.

Jesus' followers spread his teachings all over the Roman world. Many Roman citizens became Christians.

Chapter 18

Christianity and the Fall of Rome

The Romans were the first people to have a strong central government. Many Roman laws are still used in Europe today. But the Romans had also learned a lot from the Greeks. They built buildings like the Greek buildings. They wrote stories that were very much like the old Greek stories. Their art and many of their ways of living were copied (KOP-eed) from the Greeks. Educated Romans knew the works of Plato and Aristotle.

Roman religion worshipped the old Greek gods. The people began to worship other gods too. But no matter what gods a Roman of the Empire believed in, he had to worship before a statue of an emperor. The law of Rome even said that some emperors were gods. Caesar and Augustus were said to be god-emperors. There were many others.

Many Hebrews lived in cities in the Roman Empire. Their religion said they must worship one god — Jehovah (jih-HO-vuh). They would not worship the Roman emperors.

While Augustus was emperor of Rome, Jesus was born in Palestine, which was then a Roman province. Jesus was a Hebrew. He was also a preacher with many followers. During the time Tiberius (ty-BEER-ee-us) was emperor of Rome, Jesus was put to death for his teachings.

After his death, the teachings of Jesus were spread all over the Roman world. Jesus' followers traveled the Roman roads to all the cities of the Empire. They told of the new **Christian** (KRIS-chun) religion. Many Roman citizens became **Christians**.

The **Christian** religion spread into the city of Rome. As the number of **Christians** grew, the government became afraid they would try to take over the Empire. Because they feared them, some of the Roman emperors were very cruel to **Christians**. They fed hundreds of them to wild animals in the Colosseum. The **Christians** lived in fear of the government because they knew they would be treated unjustly. Many had to hide in great tunnels they dug under the city of Rome.

The more the emperors tried to stop the new religion, the more **Christians** there were every year. Even many rich people became **Christians**. Finally a Roman emperor became a **Christian** too. His name was Constantine (KON-stan-teen). He made Christianity (kris-chee-AN-ih-tee) the religion of Rome. After this life finally became safe for the **Christians**.

Constantine built a new city far to the east of Rome. It was right where Europe and Asia come together. This was a perfect place for trade. He named the city Constantinople (kon-stant-un-O-pull). Constantinople became one of the most important cities of the world.

After Constantine's death, the Roman Empire was divided into two parts to make it easier to govern. The eastern Roman Empire had its capital at Constantinople. The western Roman Empire had its capital at Rome. Christianity remained the religion of the Romans. The eastern Empire lasted for a thousand years. But the western Empire lasted for only eighty-one years.

The western Empire grew weak. The government was still not honest. Its citizens did not want to be in the army. It became easy for the Germans who lived north of Italy to attack this part of the Roman Empire. These peoples were not as civilized as the Romans. They attacked Roman cities and destroyed everything.

In the year A.D. 410, Germans entered the city of Rome. It had been eight hundred years since an enemy had marched into Rome. There was no army to stop them. For three days they robbed and burned the city. In the year A.D. 476, the last Roman emperor of the western Empire was removed. He was replaced by a German. The Senate sent the crown of Rome to Constantinople. When this happened ancient times came to an end. Where the western Empire had been, the Roman civilization almost **disappeared** (dis-uh-PEERD). The civilization of all the ancient peoples almost **disappeared**. It would take one thousand years for the people of Europe to rediscover the Roman, the Greek, and the other ancient civilizations.

I.   **Answer these to help with your reading.**
1. From what civilization did the Romans learn many things? _____

_____

2. Who was every Roman citizen required to worship? _____

_____

Who did all Hebrews worship? _____

106

3. Who was born in Palestine while Augustus was emperor? _____

_____

4. How were the Roman emperors cruel to the Christians? _____

_____

_____

5. What Roman emperor became a Christian? _____

What new city did he build? _____

6. Name the two parts the Roman Empire was divided into after Constantine's death.

   a. _____

   b. _____

How long did each last?

   a. _____

   b. _____

7. Who attacked Rome? _____

What did they do when they attacked Roman cities? _____

_____

_____

8. In what year was the last emperor of the western Roman Empire removed?

_____

Then who ruled Rome? _____

Where did the crown of Rome go? _____

II. | **Circle True or False.**

T F   1. The Romans learned nothing from the Greeks.

T F   2. There were no Hebrews in the Roman Empire.

T F 3. The Hebrews wanted to worship the Roman emperors.

T F 4. The Hebrews worshipped Jehovah.

T F 5. Jesus was put to death when Tiberius was emperor of Rome.

T F 6. Constantine became a Christian.

T F 7. Germans invaded Rome.

T F 8. The Senate sent the crown of Rome to Germany.

III. **Use one of the two vocabulary words from the beginning of this chapter to complete each of the sentences below.**

1. A person who believes in Jesus Christ and his teachings is called

   a _____.

2. When something passes from sight, it is said to _____ .

IV. **Think about and discuss in class.**

Romans did not use the same numbers we use. Our numbers come from the Arabs and are called Arabic numerals. The Romans used Roman numerals. Roman numerals are used only for special things today.

What is one use they have in this book? _____

_____

Below is a list of some Roman numerals.

I	=	1	C	=	100
V	=	5	D	=	500
X	=	10	M	=	1000
L	=	50			

When you read a Roman numeral, you must *add* equal or smaller numerals as you read from left to right.

III = 1 + 1 + 1, or 3

VIII = 5 + 1 + 1 + 1, or 8

XV = 10 + 5, or _____

But if a smaller numeral comes in front of a larger one, you must *subtract* the smaller numeral from the larger numeral as you read from left to right.

IV = 1 from 5, or 4

IX = 1 from 10, or 9

XIV = 10 + (1 from 5) 4, or _____

See if you can read the year below. What happened in this year?

C D L X X V I _____

Do you know the year Columbus discovered America?

M C D X C I I _____

See if you and your classmates can figure how the Romans would write the year it is now. _____

Try writing the year of your birth in Roman numerals. _____

Greek temples built on the Acropolis still stand. Although many are in ruins, the beauty of their statues and columns is clear.

Tombs still line the old Roman roads.

Much of the ancient art was removed from Greece by archeologists and art collectors. A museum near you probably has some Greek statues or pottery.

19 Getting Ready For Chapter Nineteen

Here are three vocabulary words that are used in the story about the importance of Italy and Greece today. Use your dictionary and write a good definition of each to show that you understand the meaning.

1. tourist: _____

_____

2. climate: _____

_____

3. natural resource: _____

_____

Chapter 19

The Importance of Italy and Greece Today

Today Italy is a modern country in Europe. In the northern part of the country there are large industrial cities. The factories there make such things as television sets, computers and cars. The Italian Fiat automobile is popular all over Europe as well as here in the United States.

North of the industrial cities are the Alps. These high mountains separate Italy from the rest of Europe. People all over Europe go to the Alps for skiing and other winter sports. Even during the summer the Alps attract people who want to get away from the city for a vacation. Today, the mountains that Hannibal bravely crossed have modern highways to make travel easier.

The capital city of Rome is still very important in Italy. Everywhere in the city there are remains of the old buildings. These buildings were used as models for public buildings in the United States. Courthouses, state capitols and federal buildings have been built in the ancient Roman style. The people who built them believed this showed their concern for strong law and order.

The leader of the Roman Catholic church, the pope lives in a special part of Rome called the Vatican (VAT-ih-kan). Roman Catholics from around the world visit the Vatican. They come to worship in the large church called Saint Peter's. On church holidays, they hope to get a view of the pope.

Throughout Italy there are reminders of ancient Rome. Old Roman aqueducts (AK-wuh-dukts) that are still in use can be seen. Along the old roads of Italy are many tombs. The Romans liked to bury their dead along the roadsides. Now **tourists** (TOOR-ists) travel the old Roman roads. They visit the old as well as the new in Italy.

Many **tourists** come to Italy every year. Some of them come to see the ruins. The old Roman forum is a favorite place they visit. **Tourists** visit the Colosseum and the Circus Maximus and try to imagine what they were like when Rome was a great city. Others come to Italy for the **climate** (KLY-mut). The southern part of Italy has sunny, warm weather, even in the winter.

Greece is a smaller country than Italy and does not have many industrial cities. Athens is still the capital of Greece. High on the Acropolis overlooking that city, ruins of the temples still stand.

Life in Greece today is simpler than life in most of Europe. There are few factories to provide work for the people. Most Greeks live as farmers. Greece has

Italy now has many factories that make such things as cars and computers. People often visit Italy to ski in the Alps.

The ruins of many of the old Roman buildings still stand in Rome. People often visit this old city just to see these ruins.

few **natural resources** (NACH-u-rul REE-sor-sez) and is not a wealthy country.

What Greece does have is beautiful weather and beautiful scenery. **Tourists** and the business they bring are a large source of income for the Greeks. Near Greece are hundreds of tiny islands in the Aegean Sea. They are very beautiful and very peaceful. These islands have become a favorite spot for **tourists**.

During World War I and World War II the city of Athens was bombed. The temples on the Acropolis were damaged. Greece is too poor to spend money to fix old temples. Other countries have spent much to save the Acropolis. Some of the statues and parts of the temples have been taken to other countries. Many are in a museum in London, England. There may even be Greek statues in a museum near where you live. Greek art, buildings, and statues are copied everywhere.

Present-day Italy and present-day Greece are not the great countries they once were. **Tourists** visit them to see what is left of the earlier civilizations. Others study them to learn more about the Greek and Roman ways of life. Perhaps some day you too will visit these countries to see what is left of these old civilizations.

I.

Answer these to help with your reading.

1. Name some things that are made in the northern cities of Italy. _____

_____

2. What city is now capital of Italy? _____

   What is the name of the special city within the city of Rome? _____

_____

3. What city is capital of Greece today? _____

4. What happened to the temples on the Acropolis during World War I and

   World War II? _____

_____

5. Why has Greece spent little money to fix the old temples? _____

_____

6. What has happened to many of the Greek statues and temples? _____

_____

_____

_____

II. **Circle the right word or words to complete each sentence below.**
1. The pope is the leader of

    a. the Roman army   b. the Roman   c. all Italy
                                       Catholic church

2. Along the Roman roads are many

    a. tombs   b. factories   c. temples

3. Many Greek statues and parts of Greek temples are in a museum in

    a. Los Angeles   b. Rome   c. London

III. **Circle True or False.**
T F 1. The Colosseum and the Circus Maximus are still visited today.

T F 2. Tourists can no longer walk on the old Roman roads.

T F 3. Italy today produces cars, TV sets and computers.

T F 4. Greece has many factories and many natural resources.

IV. **Use one of the three vocabulary words from the beginning of this chapter to complete each sentence below.**
1. A person who travels to see the sights is a _____ .

2. The minerals in the earth are part of a country's _____

    _____ .

3. The kind of weather a place has is its _____ .

The Mediterranean Sea and the Lands Near it Today

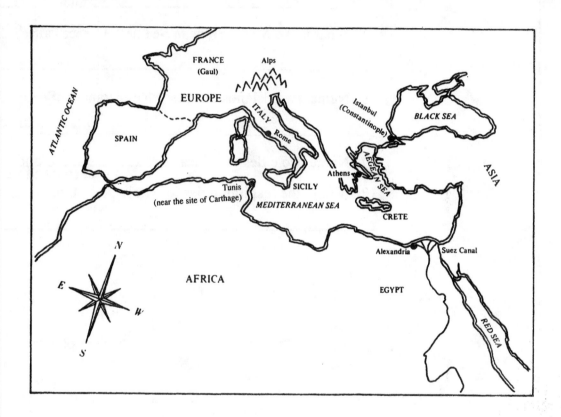

Using the map above, write answers to these questions.

1. Name the ocean that connects with the Mediterranean Sea. _____

_____

2. What two seas are connected to the Mediterranean Sea? _____

and _____

3. What mountains separate Italy from the rest of Europe? _____

_____

4. By what name is the city of Constantinople known today? _____

_____

5. What is the old Roman name for France? _____

6. Name the three continents that border on the Mediterranean Sea.

_____ , _____ and _____

7. What is the Mediterranean Sea near Greece called? _____

_____

8. Name two islands in the Mediterranean Sea. _____ and

_____

9. Name two cities of Africa. _____ and _____

10. Name the capital cities of Italy and Greece. _____ and

_____

A Test

Greece and Rome Build Great Civilizations

Each answer is worth two points. Part V is worth six points.

I.

Here is a list of fifteen vocabulary words you have learned while reading this book. Use the right word to complete each sentence below the list. Be sure you spell the word right.

Acropolis	republic	gladiator	empire	oath
bard	Christian	natural resources	textile	senate
successor	dictator	ally	myth	drama

1. A woven fabric or material is called a _____ .

2. An old story which tells of people and events that may have happened and which shows how people looked at life is known as a _____ .

3. A poet who writes or sings of heroes and their deeds is known as a _____ .

4. A large land of many nations under one ruler is called an _____ .

5. The high hill above Athens on which the Greeks built temples is the _____ .

6. A solemn promise is an _____ .

7. A play to be performed in a theater or on television is known as a _____ .

8. A person who becomes ruler after his parent's death is called the parent's _____ .

9. A body of chosen lawmakers can be called a _____ .

10. Any country that is the friend of another country so that both countries can be safer from enemies is an _____ .

11. A nation or state without a ruler, where citizens elect officials, is a _____ .

12. A Roman slave or prisoner of war who fought in the Colosseum was called a _____ .

13. One-person rule is carried out by a _____ .

14. A person who believes in Jesus Christ and his teachings is called a _____ .

15. The minerals in the earth are part of a country's _____ .

II.   **Choose the right word or words to complete each sentence below. Write just the letter on the line in front of the sentence.**

_____ 1. The story of the Minotaur is

     a. an Egyptian story   b. a news story   c. a Greek myth

_____ 2. The most famous Greek stories were told by Homer, a bard who was

     a. tall   b. blind   c. Persian

_____ 3. For their gods, the Greeks built many

     a. temples   b. cities and towns   c. churches

_____ 4. The marketplace in Greece was called the

     a. forum   b. store   c. agora

_____ 5. Socrates, Plato, and Aristotle were Greek

     a. philosophers   b. kings   c. actors

_____ 6. The country north of Greece ruled by Philip was called

     a. Athens   b. Macedonia   c. Persia

_____ 7. Philip's son Alexander wanted to spread the Greek civilization

     a. to Rome   b. to Europe   c. everywhere

_____ 8. The peninsula of Italy is shaped like a

    a. football   b. wheel   c. boot

_____ 9. A Roman myth says that the founder of Rome was

    a. Romulus   b. Remus   c. Alexander

_____ 10. The general of Carthage who crossed the Alps with his army was

    a. Alexander   b. Caesar   c. Hannibal

_____ 11. The marketplace in the city of Rome was called the

    a. agora   b. forum   c. senate

_____ 12. When Julius Caesar took control of all Rome

    a. the Roman   b. he wanted to   c. his enemies
      republic ended   change the   murdered
                            government   his son

_____ 13. The great Hebrew teacher who was born in a Roman province was

    a. Constantine   b. Augustus   c. Jesus Christ

_____ 14. Historians say that when Rome fell, it was the end of

    a. modern times   b. ancient times   c. humankind

III.   **Circle True or False.**

T F 1. The Minoans built their civilization on the island of Crete.

T F 2. The Minotaur was kept in a cage.

T F 3. The Greek city-states were always friendly and united.

T F 4. The *Iliad* is the story of the Greek war with Troy.

T F 5. Even now, the Olympic Games are held every four years.

T F 6. The Roman republic was ruled by the Senate.

T F 7. Carthage finally defeated Rome in the Punic Wars.

T F 8. The Emperor Constantine made Christianity the religion of the Roman Empire.

IV. Match the words in the first column with the right definition in the second column. Draw a line between each word and its meaning. Be careful that your answers make sense.

Column A	Column B
Zeus ●	● the large temple on the Acropolis
Hippocrates ●	● the sea around Greece
Parthenon ●	● a 26-mile-long race
Romulus and Remus ●	● great general of Carthage
Alexander ●	● the father of medicine
Aegean Sea ●	● "the Great"
Augustus ●	● founded Constantinople
Marathon ●	● twins fed by a she-wolf
Constantine ●	● the greatest of the Greek gods
Hannibal ●	● changed from "Octavian"

V. In your own words and in complete sentences, tell as many things as you can remember that the modern world got from the Greek and Roman civilizations. (Look back through this book to help your memory.) This answer is worth six points. Be sure to do your *best* work.

_____

_____

_____

_____

_____

_____

More sew-it-yourself
Home Décor

More sew-it-yourself
Home Décor

Over 50 easy-to-make designs for beds,
chairs, tables and windows

Chris Jefferys

KP Books

First published in North America in 2005 by KP Books

kp books
An imprint of F+W Publications, Inc.

700 East State Street • Iola, WI 54990-0001
715-445-2214 • 888-457-2873

Our toll-free number to place an order or obtain a
free catalog is (800) 258-0929

First published in 2005 by New Holland Publishers (UK) Ltd
London • Cape Town • Sydney • Auckland
www.newhollandpublishers.com
Garfield House, 86–88 Edgware Road
London W2 2EA, United Kingdom

ISBN 0-87349-803-8

Library of Congress Catalog Number: 2004113045

Senior Editor: Clare Sayer
Photographer: Shona Wood
Design: Frances de Rees
Illustrations: Coral Mula
Copyeditor: Patsy North
Production: Hazel Kirkman
Editorial Direction: Rosemary Wilkinson

Reproduction by Modern Age Repro, Hong Kong
Printed and bound by Times Offset (M) Sdn Bhd, Malaysia

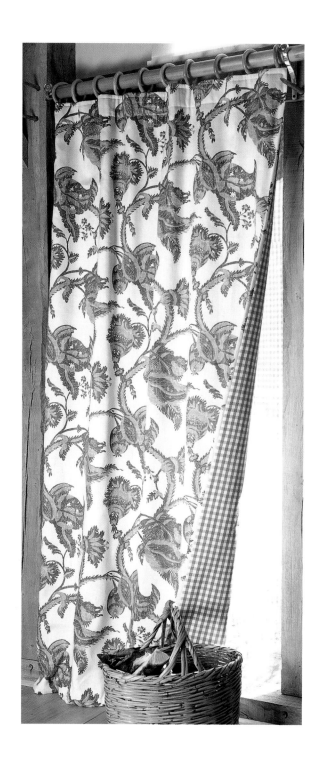

Contents

Introduction

Soft furnishings are a quick and easy way to change or update the color scheme of a room. It could be the simplest thing – a drape around the window, a throw over a sofa and some new cushions will do the trick in next to no time. There are of course some more complex soft furnishing projects where the wide choice of fabrics available will make it possible to change to a new color scheme at a fraction of the cost of buying ready-made items. By making your own soft furnishings, you have the reward of designing and creating your own look to suit your taste and lifestyle and the chance to work with a wonderful array of fabric colors and textures. The projects in this book vary from simple cushions and bedcovers to more sophisticated bolsters and fitted covers, so there is always an option for the beginner as well as the more experienced stitcher. For those new to making their own soft furnishings, there is a basics section that includes step-by-step colour photographs to take you through all the techniques needed to complete the projects successfully, from basic pinning to inserting zippers and trimming with piping.

The projects are designed for maximum style combined with simplicity: If there is an easy way to create a look, you'll find it here. The book is divided into sections

according to how the items are to be used. The Chairs section contains stylish cushions, luxurious throws and gorgeous seat covers that are easy to make and elegant.

In Tables, there are tablecloths, both round and square, with a choice of lovely decorative edges, a great napkin collection and elegant table runners to add style to the smartest table settings.

The Beds section has a full selection of pillowcase and duvet designs, an amazingly simple canopy and bedhead, and a straightforward but stunning patchwork quilt as well as valances and bedcovers.

The Windows chapter combines a wonderful array of window treatments with easy-to-make, almost no-sew drapes, and lined and unlined curtains that use tab tops and clip tops as well as conventional headings. I have included quick ways to line curtains and make pelmets as well as the more traditional methods. There are roller blinds and Roman blinds, including a really quick method which does away with all those battens and rings.

Whatever your level of experience, I am sure you find will plenty of inspiration and essential practical advice in the projects that follow.

Materials and equipment

BASIC SEWING EQUIPMENT
Dressmaker's scissors
Bent-handled dressmaker's scissors or shears are the most comfortable to use for cutting fabric accurately as the angle of the handle allows the fabric to lie flat.

Dressmaking pins
Pins are available with metal, glass or pearlized heads. Pins with colored heads are easier to spot and pick up, though selecting pins which are fine and sharp is the main importance. Extra-fine pins are available for lace.

Erasable marker
Air-erasable and water-erasable marker pens are easily available and are a useful addition to your sewing kit. Air-erasable marks will disappear after a fairly short time. Water-erasable marks will remain until touched with water.

Needles
Various types of needles are available and a mixed pack of multi-purpose needles is often the best option. Choose needles which are fine and sharp with eyes large enough to thread easily. Extra-fine needles are also available.

Ruler
A metal or plastic ruler is handy to measure and mark short distances and as a guide for drawing straight lines.

Small scissors or snips
Small sharp scissors or special snips are useful for snipping thread ends and can be used close to the fabric where larger scissors would be unwieldy.

Tape measure
A plastic-coated or cloth tape measure is used to measure longer distances and around curves. A retractable tape measure is a neat option.

HOME DECOR EQUIPMENT

Bias binding
This is a strip of fabric cut on the cross grain and comes with the edges pressed over ready for use. It is available in cotton and satin and in various widths.

Blind cord
A strong, fine cord that is threaded through the blind rings and pulled or released to raise or lower the blind.

Blind rings
Small plastic or brass rings that are stitched to the wrong side of Roman and festoon blinds as part of the lowering and raising system.

Buttons
Often made from plastic or pearl, buttons fasten through buttonholes or loops to close an opening. Fabric-covered buttons can be made by covering metal or plastic molds.

Curtain heading tape
A stiff tape available in different widths and styles that is stitched to the top of curtains and pulled up to form pleats or gathers.

Decorative trims
Tassels, rickrack, piping, and ribbons are all decorative trims that can be inserted in seams or stitched to the surface of items.

Eyelets
Chrome or brass metal rings are used to make holes in fabric to thread a pole or cord through or simply as a decorative feature.

Lining fabric
Used to line curtains when required to give extra weight and body. Lining can also be used to cover the wrong side of an item when it will not show.

Press-stud tape

A tape with snaps already attached at intervals. Used to fasten long openings such as duvet cover openings.

Thread

Multi-purpose polyester thread for use on all types of fabric is available in a wide range of colors. Cotton and silk thread is also available for use on their respective fabrics. Invisible thread is a strong nylon thread and buttonhole twist or bold thread is a thicker, stronger thread, useful for handsewing heavier fabrics.

Velcro

A fastener that comes in two parts, with hooks on one and soft loops on the other, which stick together when closed. Available in strip form or spots and for sewing or sticking on.

Zippers

These are fasteners with metal or plastic teeth that interlock together when the zipper tag is pulled over them. Used widely in openings for cushion covers.

THE SEWING MACHINE

Most sewing machines are run by electricity through a foot pedal, which is attached by one cable to the machine and another to the electricity supply. Pressure on the foot pedal will start the machine going and, as more pressure is added, the speed will increase. A hand wheel at the right of the machine is also usually employed when starting and stopping a piece of machine-stitching to help control and smooth the process.

Machine-stitching is formed from two threads: the top thread and the bobbin thread. Thread is first wound from the thread reel onto the bobbin by a system usually situated on the top of the machine. The top thread is then slotted through a number of guides and down and through the needle. The wound bobbin is placed into the bobbin case, which is under the needle. During the stitching process, the top thread forms the stitch on the top of the fabric, and the bobbin thread forms the stitch on the underside, with the two interlinking within the fabric.

Needles for sewing machines come in a variety of different sizes. The lower the number, the finer the needle point.

Basic techniques

This section takes you through all the essential techniques needed to complete the projects in this book, from pinning and tacking to more advanced techniques such as piping. Once mastered, the basics will be used again and again to complete rewarding projects.

Pinning, tacking and handstitches

PINNING AND TACKING
Crossways pinning
Place the edges to be joined together and pin the two layers together with pins at right angles to the edge. Place the pins about 5 cm (2 in) apart; on firm fabric, you can space them further apart. Pin diagonally at corners.

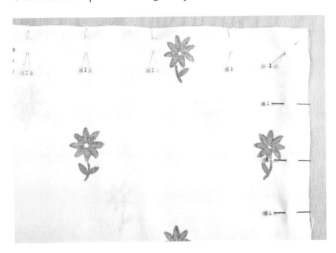

Lengthways pinning
Lengthways pins are placed along the seamline where it will be stitched. This method can be more effective in tricky areas such as fitting a curved edge to a straight edge. When tacking or stitching, remove these pins as you reach them.

Pinning hems
Hems can be pinned with crossways pins or with pins lying in the same direction as the inner fold of the hem. Crossways pins are more effective if any fullness is being eased in, such as on a curved hem. Remove the pins when tacking or stitching, in the same way as before.

Tacking
Using sewing thread or special tacking thread, begin and finish tacking with one or two backstitches. Tack by stitching in and out through the layers of fabric, making stitches 1–1.5 cm ($^3/_8$–$^5/_8$ in) long. Work the tacking over crossways pins and remove the pins afterwards. Or, on lengthways pinning, remove the pins as you reach them.

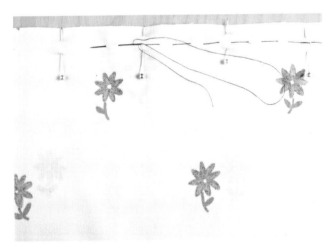

HANDSTITCHES

Backstitches

These stitches are worked one on top of the other and are used to start and finish handstitching. When tacking, the stitches can be 6 mm ($\frac{1}{4}$ in) long. In other areas, it is best to make them as small as possible and position them where they are least noticeable. Insert the needle into the fabric and out again, return the needle to the beginning and work two or three more stitches on top of the first one.

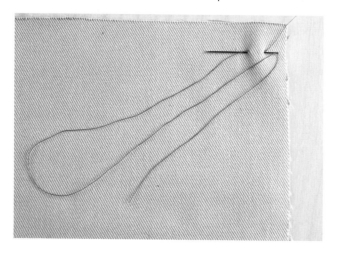

Slip hem

Used to stitch hems and the inner edge of bias binding. Begin with backstitches near the fold of the hem. Stitch across to pick up just a thread of fabric above the hem, then stitch along diagonally back through the hem again. Repeat, taking care not to pull too tight. When stitching binding, instead of picking up a fabric thread the stitch can pass through the back of the machine stitching.

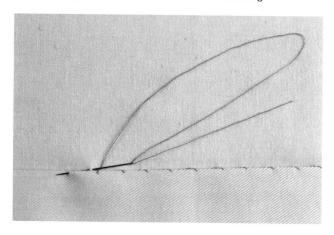

Slipstitch

This stitch is used to sew lining to curtains. Make each stitch about 1.5 cm ($\frac{5}{8}$ in) long. Slide the needle along under the main fabric then out to pick up a couple of threads at the edge of the lining. Take the needle back to the main fabric and slide it along again to make the next stitch.

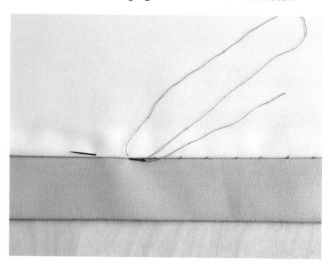

Ladder stitch

This is used to stitch two butting folded edges together. Start with backstitches, then take the needle along inside the fold of one edge for about 3–6 mm ($\frac{1}{8}$–$\frac{1}{4}$ in). Bring the needle out at the fold, take it directly across to the other fold edge, and stitch along inside that fold in the same way. Repeat.

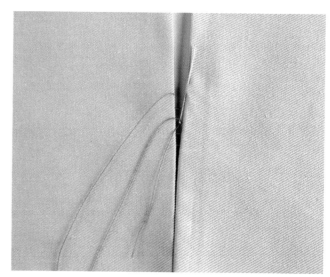

Blanket stitch

A decorative stitch, used to finish the edges of blankets and throws on fabrics that do not fray. Work from left to right. Begin with backstitches on the wrong side and bring the needle out to the right side about 12 mm–1.5 cm ($\frac{1}{2}$–$\frac{5}{8}$ in) in from the edge. Moving the needle along about 12 mm ($\frac{1}{2}$ in), take it through to the wrong side and downwards so that its point projects beyond the fabric edge. Loop the thread under the needle, then pull the needle through. Repeat. At each corner, work three stitches into the same hole as shown.

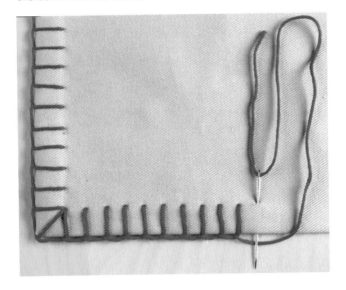

Long stitch

This is used to stitch the side hems on interlined curtains where it holds the hem to the interlining. Make a horizontal stitch across from right to left, then take the needle down diagonally for about 4 cm ($1\frac{1}{2}$ in) and repeat.

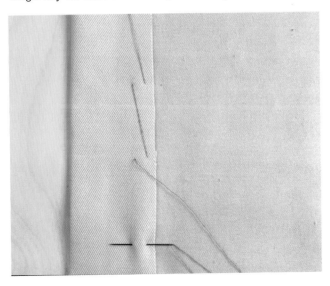

Herringbone stitch

Used to stitch hems on interlined curtains and to join butted edges of wadding and interlining. Work from left to right and begin with backstitches. Bring the needle through the hem, take it diagonally up to the right, and take a stitch through above the hem from right to left. Bring the needle diagonally down to the right and take a stitch through the hem again from right to left. Repeat.

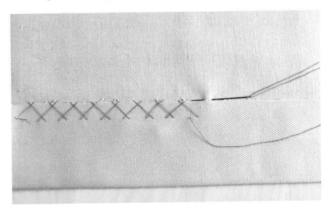

Lockstitch

Used to stitch interlining to curtain fabric on interlined curtains. Fold back the interlining at the required position. Begin with back stitches on the interlining, then move the needle along and take a stitch through the fold of the interlining. Leave a loop of thread between the previous stitch and the needle eye and take a small stitch to pick up the curtain fabric within this loop. Pull the stitch through but do not pull it tight. Space the stitches at intervals of about 10 cm (4 in).

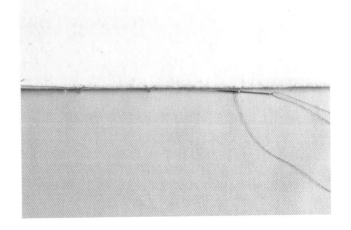

Seams and hems

Whether you tack as well as pin your fabrics together before machining is a matter of personal preference. The less experienced may wish to pin and tack before stitching, while those with more confidence may prefer just to pin and remove the pins as the stitching reaches them.

Plain seam

A plain seam is used to join two pieces of fabric together. It can be pressed open when joining widths of fabric or left with the edges together, such as around the edge of a cushion. The seam allowance is usually 1.5 cm ($^{5}/_{8}$ in) wide. If it varies, this will be stated in the instructions.

1 Place the fabric pieces together with right sides facing and raw edges level. Stitch along 1.5 cm ($^{5}/_{8}$ in) in from the edge.

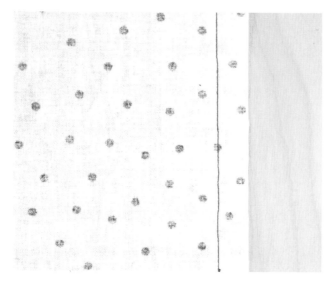

2 Open out the fabric and press the seam open, using the point of the iron. If the raw edges are exposed, zigzag stitch along each edge to neaten.

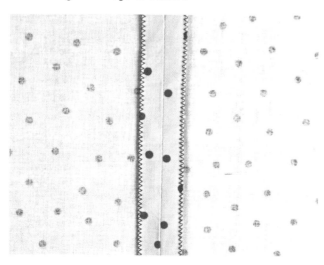

Narrow seam

This type of seam is used on sheer fabrics, as it is neater and less noticeable than a seam pressed open.
Stitch the seam as for a Plain seam, step 1. Trim both seam allowances together to about half their original width. Zigzag stitch the two raw edges together. Open out the fabric and press the seam to one side.

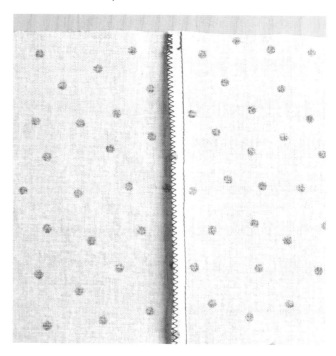

Trimming and snipping

The seam allowances are usually left intact, but if they cause too much bulk at the edge of an item, they can be trimmed to about half their original width.

Outer corners First make a diagonal cut across the corner, then cut away wedges from either side of the diagonal cut.

Inner corners On an internal corner, snip into the corner to a few threads from the stitching, but take care not to snip too close to the stitching.

Curves On a concave curve, snip into the seam allowance so that the seam allowance can expand when turned right side out. On a convex curve, cut out small wedge-shaped notches. The tighter the curve, the closer together the notches and snips should be.

Flat fell seam

A flat fell seam is used to join fabrics where a strong, easy-to-launder seam is required.

1 Place the two edges together with wrong sides facing and raw edges level. Stitch 1.5 cm ($^{5}/_{8}$ in) in from the edge. Trim one seam allowance to 6 mm ($^{1}/_{4}$ in).

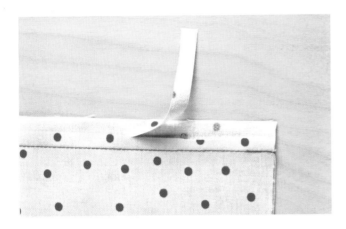

2 Open out the fabric and press the seam so the wider seam allowance lies on top of the trimmed one. Tuck the wider seam allowance under the trimmed edge and press. Stitch along close to the pressed fold by machine. The finished seam will have two rows of machine stitching on the right side.

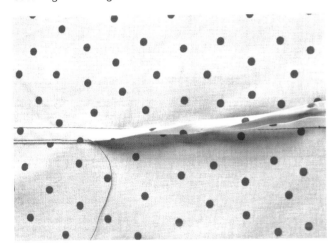

Basic hem

Press 1–1.5 cm ($\frac{3}{8}$–$\frac{5}{8}$ in) to the wrong side, then press the hem depth to the wrong side and stitch in place by hand or machine.

Double hem

This type of hem is used on sheer fabrics to conceal the inner layer of the hem.

First press the hem depth to the wrong side, then press the same amount again and stitch in place by hand or machine.

Blind hemstitched hem

Most machines have a blind hemstitch, which consists of a few straight stitches followed by a wide zigzag stitch. The straight stitches are worked along the hem edge and the zigzag stitch catches the hem to the main fabric. The stitch can be fiddly to set up accurately, but is worth the effort when stitching long lengths.

Form the hem as described above. Then, with the wrong side facing up, fold back the hem under the main fabric with the hem edge projecting and stitch in place.

Bias binding and piping

BIAS BINDING

Bias binding can be bought or made. To make your own bias strips for both binding and covering piping cord, cut strips four times the required finished width diagonally across the fabric. For binding, then press both long edges in so that they almost meet at the center.

Joining strips

1 Open the binding folds and trim the two ends on the straight grain. Place the two ends together with right sides facing, the straight ends level and the foldlines intersecting 6 mm (¼ in) in. Pin to hold. Stitch the two ends together, taking a 6 mm (¼ in) seam.

2 Open the binding and press the seam open. Trim off the corners of the seam level with the edge of the binding and re-press the binding folds.

Binding an edge

1 Unfold one edge of the binding and place the raw edge level with the fabric edge on the right side of the fabric. Stitch in place along the fold.

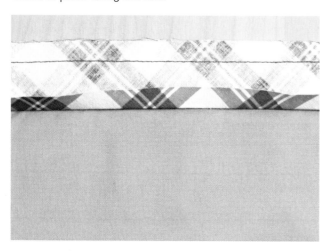

2 Fold the other edge of the binding over to the wrong side so that its edge is level with the machine stitching and stitch in place by hand.

Sandwich method

Before stitching, fold and press the binding in half lengthways so that the upper half, which will be on the right side, is slightly narrower than the lower half. Sandwich the fabric into the binding and stitch in place from the right side.

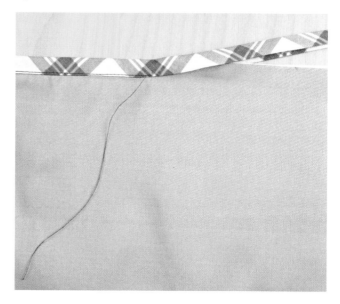

Double binding method

This is a neat method for lighter-weight fabrics and wider bindings.

1 Cut the bias strip six times the required finished width and press the binding in half lengthways. Place the raw edges level with the fabric edge on the wrong side and stitch in place the required width of the binding in from the edge.

2 Fold the other edge over to the right side so that it just covers the stitching and machine-stitch in place.

Joining ends

Join the ends with a diagonal seam before the stitching is complete, using the same method as for joining lengths of bias binding.

Alternatively, an easier method is to overlap the finishing end over the starting end, tucking the raw end under as shown, and then complete the stitching.

Using bought bias binding

Ready-made bias binding can be found in a range of colors and is also available with a satin finish as well as in plain cotton. It is also available in a variety of widths and some speciality fabric stores will have patterned bias binding (see Roller blind with scalloped border, page 144). It comes ready folded and is attached in the same way as for homemade binding strips.

PIPING

Piping can be bought ready-made with a projecting flange to insert into a seam or it can be made by covering piping cord with a strip of bias-cut fabric.

Stitching piping

1 Cut the bias strip wide enough to fit around the cord plus two seam allowances of 1.5 cm (⅝ in). Wrap the strip around the cord and, using a zipper foot, stitch along close to the cord but not right next to it.

2 Place the piping onto the right side of one fabric layer and stitch in place along the line of the first stitching.

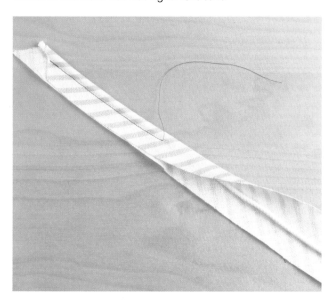

3 Sandwich the piping with the other layer of the seam. Then turn the piece over so that the previous stitching is facing up. Stitch in place just inside the previous stitching so that the first two rows will be hidden.

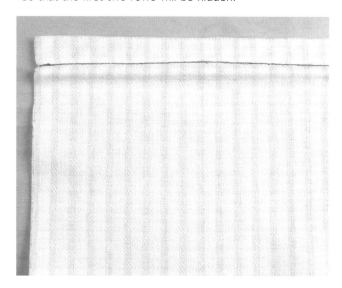

Piping around a corner

Snip the flat flange 1.5 cm (⅝ in) in from the corner so that it will open out to fit around the corner, ensuring that the raw edges are level with the next edge. If the corner is curved, make three snips around it.

Joining piping ends, method one

1 Leave about 2.5 cm (1 in) unstitched at each end of the piping. Cut the piping so that it overlaps the first end by 2 cm (³⁄₄ in). Unpick the end of the piping to reveal the cord and snip away the cord only, so that it butts up to the beginning of the cord.

2 Fold under 1 cm (³⁄₈ in) on the overlapping end of the piping and lap it over the beginning of the piping. Then complete the stitching, overlapping the beginning of the stitching line.

Joining piping ends, method two

With this method, the ends of the piping are overlapped at an angle and finished inside the seam. This method can also be used for purchased piping where it is not possible to cut away the inner piping cord. In this case, press the overlapped ends as flat as possible before stitching across them.

Leave the piping unstitched for 2.5 cm (1 in) on each side of the join and allow some excess at each end of the piping. Overlap the ends at the seamline, unpick the fabric covering and trim the cords where they overlap. Replace the covering and overlap the flat ends diagonally into the seam allowance. Then complete the stitching, overlapping the beginning of the stitching line.

Fringing and frills

FRINGING

Fringing can be purchased as a trim or made by pulling away the threads from a woven fabric. Some woven fabrics do not fringe well, so check before purchasing.

Applying fringing trim

1 Press a narrow hem, just wide enough to be covered by the braid part of the fringe, onto the right side.

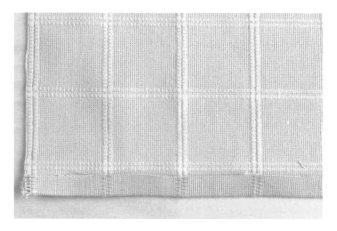

2 Lay the fringing braid along the hem to cover it. Stitch in place with a row of stitching near the fabric edge and another just above the raw edge so that it is enclosed.

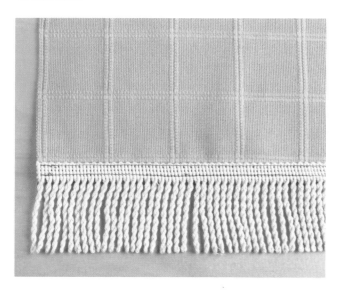

Fringing fabric

A fringe can be made by simply pulling the fabric threads away from the fabric edge. For a more durable fringe, particularly on items that will be laundered, first stitch a row of narrow zigzag stitching in a matching color across the fabric at the top of the fringe. Then fringe the fabric back to the stitching.

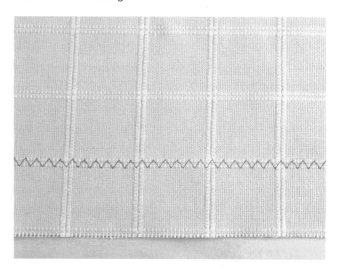

Knotting and plaiting

Both knotting and plaiting will reduce the length of a fringe considerably, so, whenever possible, test on a piece of spare fabric.

To knot, simply gather a bunch of threads together and knot them near the top of the fringe.

For a plait, gather a bunch in the same way, divide it into three sections and plait together. Finish near the base with a thread wrapped round and round and knotted firmly.

FRILLS

Frills can be made from a single layer of fabric with a hemmed edge or from fabric folded double so that no hem is needed. The frills shown here are gathered, but they could be pleated instead. A lace frill can be attached in the same way. For a gathered frill, allow 1½ times the length of the edge it will be trimming.

Single frill

1 Cut the frill to the required width plus 12 mm (½ in) for the hem and 1.5 cm (⅝ in) seam allowance. Press 6 mm (¼ in), then another 6 mm (¼ in) to the wrong side along one long edge of the frill and stitch in place. If the ends will show, hem them in the same way.

2 Adjust the machine stitch to its longest length and stitch along 1.5 cm (⅝ in) from the other edge. Stitch a second row of gathering 6 mm (¼ in) inside the first row. On long frills, stop and restart the stitching to divide the gathered edge up into about 75 cm (30 in) lengths.

3 Divide the frill and the edge to which it will be stitched into an equal number of sections and mark with pins. With right sides facing, pin the edges together at the marker pins. Pull the gathering threads on the wrong side of the frill together while sliding the fabric along to form gathers.

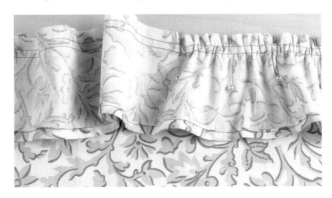

4 When gathered to fit, wind the thread ends around a pin in a figure-eight to hold. Adjust the gathers evenly and stitch in place just below the inner row of gathers.

Double frill

Cut the frill twice the required finished width plus 3 cm (1¼ in). If the ends will show, fold the frill in half with right sides together, stitch across the ends, then turn the frill right sides out. Press the frill in half lengthways with the right sides outside. Gather and attach the frill as for the single frill, steps 2, 3 and 4.

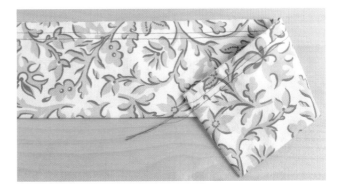

Borders and mitered borders

Block border

Used in traditional patchwork, a blocked border is stitched first to two opposite edges. The borders that are then stitched to the remaining two edges continue across the ends of the first borders. If the center panel is rectangular, stitch the two longer edges first.

Measure the first two edges and cut borders to this length by the desired finished width plus 3 cm (1¼ in). With right sides facing, stitch the borders to the center panel, taking 1.5 cm (⅝ in) seam allowances. Press the seams towards the borders. Measure the two remaining edges, including the ends of the first borders, and cut the borders to this length and the same width. Stitch in place and press in the same way as the first borders.

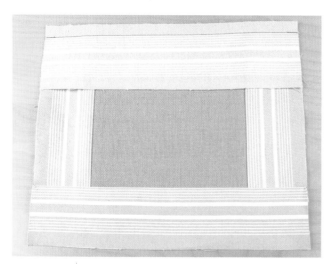

Single-mitered border

Decide on the desired finished width of the border and add on 3 cm (1¼ in). For the length, measure the length of the center panel including seam allowances and add twice the width of the finished border.
1 Mark and match the center of the borders to the center edges to which they are being stitched. Stitch the borders to the edges, starting and finishing the stitching 1.5 cm (⅝ in) in from the edge of the center panel. Stitch all the borders in this way.

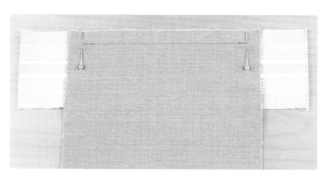

2 Fold the center panel diagonally so that two adjoining borders are level. Draw a diagonal line from the end of the previous stitching to the outer corner of the border. Stitch along the line. Trim away the corners 1 cm (⅜ in) outside the line and press the seam open. Stitch all corners in this way. Then press the panel seams toward the borders.

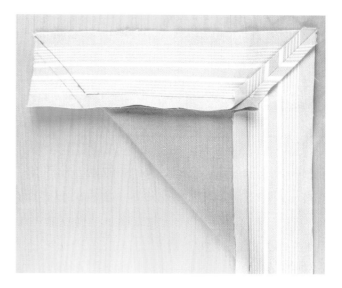

Double-mitered border

To calculate the width to cut the borders, decide on the desired finished width of the border, double this and add on 3 cm (1¼ in) seam allowances. For the length, measure the length of the center panel, including seam allowances, plus twice the width of the finished border.
1 Fold the borders in half with the wrong sides outside. Overlap the ends of two borders at right angles, with the folded edges on the outer edges and the ends projecting by 1.5 cm (⅝ in), and pin.

Draw a seam line diagonally across the corner between the points where the borders intersect. Mark the seam allowance 1 cm (⅜ in) outside the seamline. Turn the border over and repeat on the other side. Trim along the outer lines.

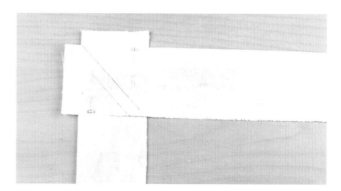

2 Unpin the borders; open them and mark the seamline on the unmarked half of each border. Place the appropriate two borders together with right sides facing and stitch along the marked lines, starting and finishing 1.5 cm ($^5/_8$ in) in from the side edges of the border. Trim the point and press the seam open. Stitch all four corners in this way.

3 Place the right side of one border edge to the wrong side of the center panel. Pin together, making sure all four corners match so that the end of the border stitching is 1.5 cm ($^5/_8$ in) from each edge at the corners. Stitch each edge separately, stopping and restarting at each corner.

4 Press the seam allowance to the wrong side along the remaining edge of the border. Then place it over to the right side of the center panel so that it just covers the previous stitching and the seam is enclosed. Stitch in place.

Mitered hem

1 Press the appropriate double hem in place, then unfold. Fold the corner over, diagonally level with the inner pressed corner. Press the fold and trim the corner away 1 cm ($^3/_8$ in) inside the fold.

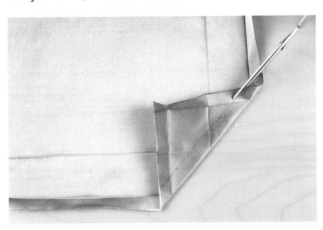

2 Refold the corners with right sides facing so that the pressed lines match. Stitch along the pressed line from the corner to finish at the outer hem fold. Press the miter seam open. Refold the hem and press again.

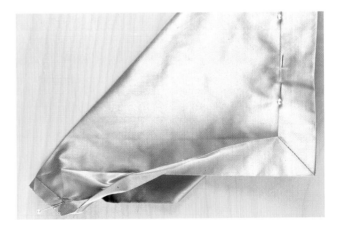

Buttons, buttonholes, ties and zippers

BUTTONS

There are two main types of buttons: flat buttons, which have two or four holes pierced through them, and shank buttons, which have a protruding shank at the back through which they are stitched on. A shank spaces the button away from the fabric to allow fabric layers to lie flat under the button when it is fastened.

Stitching on a flat button

Using a double thread, stitch a couple of backstitches, one on top of the other, at the button position. Pass the needle up through one hole, then back down through the other hole and through the fabric. Work four to six stitches in this way to secure the button. On buttons with four holes, work two parallel sets of stitches, or form the stitches into a cross, then fasten off the thread with more backstitches behind the fabric.

Making a shank for a flat button

1 Stitch on the button in the same way as for a button with holes, but work over a toothpick or thick needle placed on top of the button as a spacer.

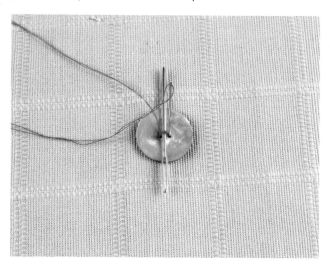

2 Before finishing off, take the thread through to between the button and the fabric. Remove the spacer and wind the thread around the stitches between the button and fabric to form a thread shank, then finish off on the reverse.

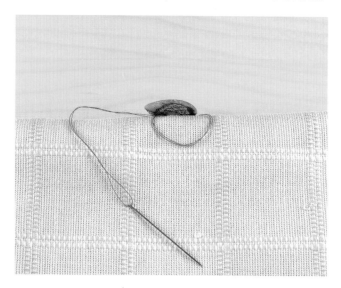

Stitching on a shank button

Using a double thread, secure the thread ends with a backstitch at the button position. Stitch alternately through the shank and the fabric four to six times, then finish off with backstitches on the wrong side behind the button.

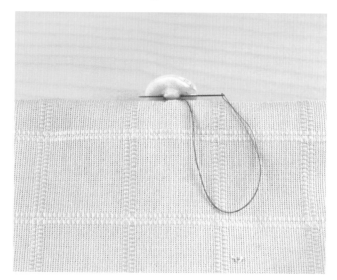

24

MAKING BUTTONHOLES

Buttonholes are quick and easy to work by machine. The exact method varies according to the machine model and will be explained in your manual.

Buttonholes are stitched with a close zigzag stitch, with wide stitches, called bar tacks, at each end and stitches half as wide along each side of the buttonhole. Cut the buttonhole along the center after stitching, using a small scissors to cut from each end towards the center.

TIES

1 Press 1 cm (³/₈ in) to the wrong side across one short end, or both ends if they are exposed, and along both long edges.

2 Fold the tie in half lengthways and press again. Stitch down the length of the tie. On wide ties, stitch across the pressed end as well. On narrow 12 mm (¹/₂ in) wide ties, the end can be left unstitched.

ZIPPERS

1 Stitch the seam at either end of the zipper position, leaving an opening the length of the zipper teeth. Press the seam open and the seam allowances to the wrong side across the opening edges. Working with right sides facing up, pin and tack the zipper behind the opening so that one edge of the opening is just outside the zipper teeth. Using a zipper foot, stitch in place near the edge.

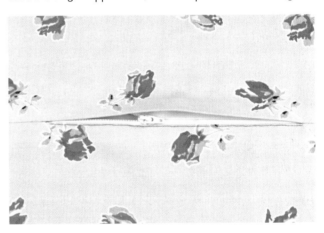

2 Arrange the other edge of the opening level with the stitching. Pin, then tack this edge to the zipper tape. Stitch in place across each end and along the tape as shown.

Pleats and tucks

PLEATS

Pleated frills and skirts make attractive trims and are a little more tailored than gathered frills and skirts. All types of pleats can be left unpressed so that the pleats are held only at the top edge, or the pleats can be pressed in place, down their length, for a more formal look.

Making knife pleats

Measure and mark the depth of the pleats at the top edge with pins or an erasable marker pen. Fold one marking over to meet the other. Pin, then tack along the seamline at the top edge. If making rows of pleats, stitch across the top edge to hold them in place.

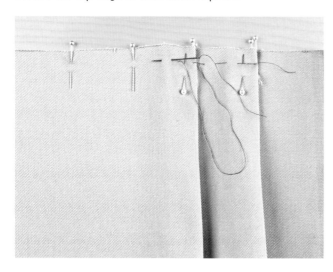

Box pleats

Box pleats are formed from two pleats facing away from each other. Measure and mark the depth of the pleats at the top edge with pins or an erasable marker pen. Fold the two inner markings outwards, away from each other, to meet the outer markings. Pin, then tack along the seamline at the top edge.

Inverted pleats

These are formed from two pleats facing towards each other so that the two folds meet at the center of the pleat. Measure and mark the depth of the pleats at the top edge with pins or an erasable marker pen. Fold the two outer markings inwards towards each other to meet at the center marking. Pin, then tack along the seamline at the top edge.

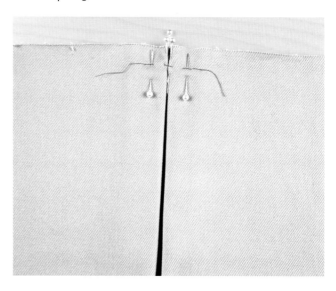

Pressed pleats

Measure and mark the pleats at intervals down the entire length of the pleat. Form the pleats and press, removing the pins as you reach them. Tack or stitch across the top edge to hold the pleats in place.

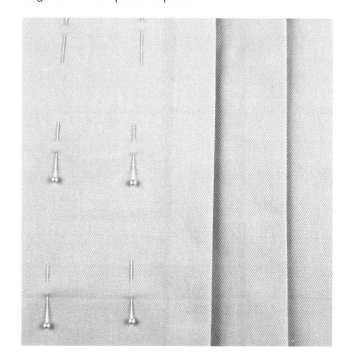

TUCKS

Tucks are stitched folds of fabric formed for a decorative effect and work particularly well with semi-sheer fabrics, as the tucks will show up well against the light. The distance of the stitching from the fold determines the type of tuck. Very fine tucks are called pin tucks. When using tucks, add twice the depth of each tuck to the fabric length.

Making pin tucks

Fold the fabric along the line of the tuck with wrong sides facing and press along the fold. With the fabric still folded, stitch along 3 mm (⅛ in) in from the fold using the machine foot as a guide. Open the fabric and press the tuck to one side. A series of parallel pin tucks are more effective than single ones.

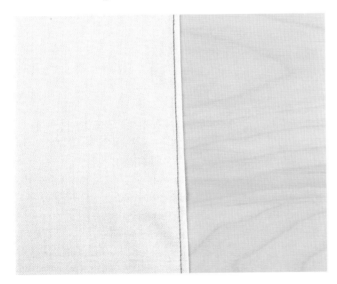

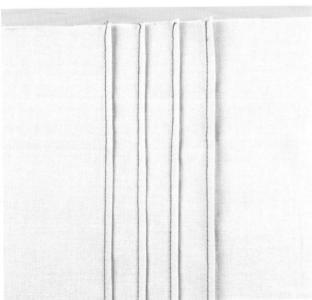

Wide tucks

Fold the fabric along the line of the tuck and press along the fold. Measure the depth of the tuck away from the fold with pins or an erasable marker pen. Tack, then stitch along the tacked line. Alternatively, stitch, keeping the fabric fold against one of the guidelines on the plate beside the machine foot to keep the stitching an even distance in from the fold. Open the fabric and press the tuck to one side.

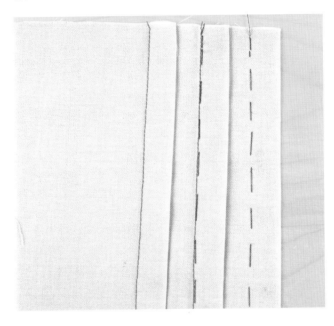

Twin needle tucks

A machine twin needle, which stitches two parallel rows, gives a fine tucked effect on light-weight fabrics such as sheer cotton or linens. First press a crease to form a line for the tuck. Open the fabric and stitch along the pressed crease so that it is central between the two needles.

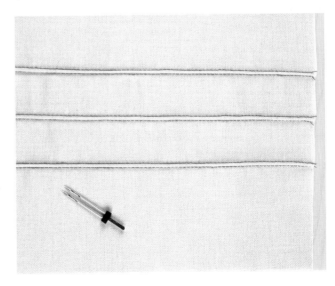

Chairs

Flap back cushion cover

This quick and easy method is ideal for square or rectangular cushions. The opening on the back of the cushion cover is formed by two overlapping edges between which the cushion pad is slipped in. Overlap the edges by 10 cm (4 in) on cushions up to 35 cm (13¾ in) square or by 15 cm (6 in) on larger cushions. For a rectangular cushion, place the overlap across the width of the cover rather than the length so that the opening does not gape.

DIAGRAM 2

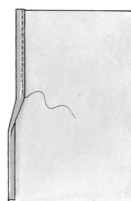

MATERIALS
Silk upholstery fabric
Sewing thread
Cushion pad

CUTTING OUT

1.5 cm (⅝ in) seam allowances are included unless instructions state otherwise.

Cut out the front to the width and length of the cushion pad plus 3 cm (1¼ in). Cut out the back to the same length and 14 cm (5½ in) wider than the front, or 19 cm (7½ in) wider for a larger cushion (diagram 1). Cut the back piece in half widthways (diagram 2).

DIAGRAM 1

1   Press a double 1 cm (⅜ in) hem to the wrong side along the center edges of the two back pieces. Stitch in place (diagram 3).

DIAGRAM 3

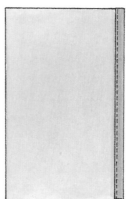

2 Place the two back pieces onto the front piece with right sides facing, arranging so that the raw edges are level all around and the hemmed edges of the back overlap. Pin together around the edge (diagram 4).

DIAGRAM 4

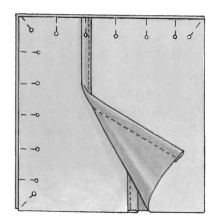

3 Stitch around the outer edge 1.5 cm ($^5/_8$ in) in from the raw edges. Trim the corners (diagram 5). Turn the cover right-side out through the overlapping edges and press. Insert the cushion pad.

DIAGRAM 5

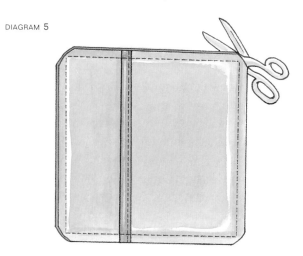

Variation

TWO-COLOR CUSHION

For this easy decorative option, cut the cushion front from two fabrics in different colors, adding 1.5 cm ($^5/_8$ in) on the edges to be joined. Join the edges with a 1.5 cm ($^5/_8$ in) plain seam and press the seam open. Using a machine straight stitch or zigzag stitch, stitch on ribbons parallel to the seam. Stitch a few beads by hand along the edge of one ribbon to complete the effect. Make up in the same way as the Flap back cushion cover, page 30.

Cushion cover with zipper

A cushion cover fastened with a zipper is a little more complicated than a flap back cover, but it has the advantage of keeping the edges of the opening pulled firmly together. You could make a feature of the zipper by placing it on the front of the cover and trimming it with beads or a tassel, or use it in a purely functional way on the back of the cover. Choose a zipper about 10 cm (4 in) shorter than the width of the cushion.

MATERIALS
Silk dupioni or other upholstery fabric
Sewing thread
Zipper
Piping (optional)
Cushion pad
Tassel

CUTTING OUT

1.5 cm ($^5/_8$ in) seam allowances are included unless instructions state otherwise.

Cut out the front to the width and height of the cushion pad plus 3 cm (1$^1/_4$ in) all round. Cut the back to the same width by the height of the pad plus 6 cm (2$^1/_2$ in).

Cut the back piece in two the required distance down from the top edge.

1 Place the two cut edges of the back pieces together with right sides facing. Stitch about 6.5 cm (2½ in) in from each end, leaving a central opening the length of the zipper teeth (diagram 1). Stitch the zipper in place, see Zippers, page 25.

DIAGRAM 1

2 Make a length of piping to fit around the cushion front and, using a piping foot, stitch it in place around the edge, see Piping, page 18.

3 Open the zipper. With right sides facing, place the front to the back. Stitch around the outer edge 1.5 cm (⅝ in) in from the raw edges, again using the piping foot if piping has been inserted. Trim the corners (diagram 2). Turn the cover right-side out through the zipper opening and press. Insert the cushion pad.

DIAGRAM 2

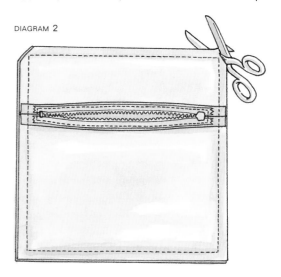

Mitered cushion cover

This cushion cover has a smart mitered border stitched around a central panel. As the border is made from separate strips, you can combine different fabrics in many imaginative ways, using subtle coordinating tones and textures or contrasting colors and patterns.

NOTE
The method shown here allows the cushion pad to fill the whole cushion cover. However, if you prefer, you could adapt the method so that the cushion fills the central panel only, leaving the mitered border to lie flat around it. Simply stitch the border to the central panel and complete the cushion as for the Flap back cushion cover, page 30. Then topstitch around the inner edge of the border.

MATERIALS
Upholstery fabric for border and back
Coordinate or contrast fabric for central panel
Sewing thread
Cushion pad

CUTTING OUT
1.5 cm (⅝ in) seam allowances are included unless instructions state otherwise.

Cut out the central panel to the desired finished size plus 3 cm (1¼ in). Cut the borders to the desired finished width plus 3 cm (1¼ in). For each border length, measure the length or width of the central panel and add on twice the finished border width.

1 Pin and stitch the borders to the central panel (diagram 1). Miter the corners, see Single mitered border, page 22.

2 Cut out two back pieces and make up the cushion cover in the same way as the Flap back cushion cover, page 32 (diagram 2). Insert the cushion pad.

DIAGRAM 1

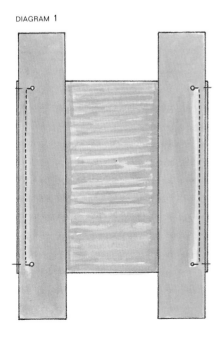

DIAGRAM 2

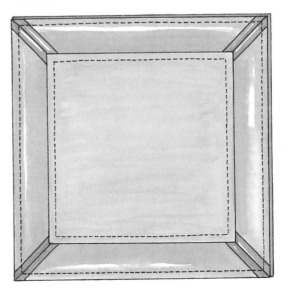

Cushion with ties

The pretty cushion is simple to make. It has a flap facing to tuck the pad behind and straight ties to hold the edges together. The facing and ties can be made from a contrasting fabric or from the same fabric as the cover.

MATERIALS
Medium-weight upholstery fabric for cushion cover
Contrasting fabric for facing and ties
Sewing thread
Cushion pad

CUTTING OUT

1.5 cm ($^5/_8$ in) seam allowances are included unless instructions state otherwise.

Cut two pieces for the cover front and back the size of the cushion pad plus 3 cm ($1^1/_4$ in). Cut two facing pieces the width of the cover by 12 cm ($4^3/_4$ in) deep. Cut four ties 18 x 8 cm (7 x $3^1/_4$ in).

1 Make the ties by folding each tie in half lengthways with right sides together and stitching across one short edge and the long edge. Trim the seams and corners, turn the ties right-side out and press.

2 Place two ties to one edge of each of the front and back pieces with the ties spaced equally and the raw edges level. Place a facing piece on top of each of the front and back pieces with right sides together and stitch together along the edge so that the ends of the ties are enclosed in the seams (diagram 1).

DIAGRAM 1

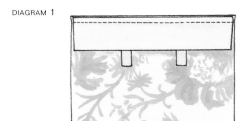

3 Open the facings away from the cushion and press the seams open. Place the front and back together with right sides together and the facing seams matching exactly. Stitch the front and back together around three sides, including the sides of the facing (diagram 2).

DIAGRAM 2

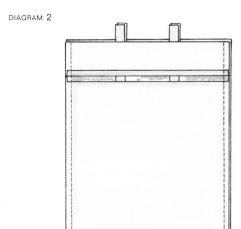

4 Trim the corners and turn the cushion cover right side out. Stitch a narrow double hem to the wrong side around the edge of the facing. Press the facing inside the cushion so that the seam is at the edge. Open the side seams and, working from the right side, stitch down each side seam through both the cover and facing to hold the facing in place (diagram 3). Insert the cushion pad.

DIAGRAM 3

Gathered-end bolster

This long, cylindrical cushion can be made with a simple, plain seam at each end, but its shape is defined more crisply if a fine piping is inserted around the seam. The circular ends are gathered and finished with a button in this version. A bolster with flat ends is given on pages 40–41. There is a zipper opening in the seam at the back of the cushion.

MATERIALS
Upholstery fabric
Sewing thread
Zipper about 7 cm (2¾ in) shorter than bolster pad
Piping cord
2 fabric-covered buttons
Bolster pad

CUTTING OUT

1.5 cm (⅝ in) seam allowances are included unless instructions state otherwise.

Measure around the circumference of the bolster pad and along the pad's length. Add on 3 cm (1¼ in) to each measurement and cut the main pieces to this size. Cut the two rectangular end pieces to the same circumference by half the diameter of the ends plus 3 cm (1¼ in).

1 Cover the piping cord with bias strips of fabric, see Piping, page 18. Place the two lengthways edges of the main piece together with right sides facing and stitch for about 5 cm (2 in) at each end, leaving an opening at the center the length of the zipper teeth. Stitch the zipper in place, taking care to keep the underlayer out of the way, see Zippers, page 25. Stitch the piping around each end of the main piece.

2 Stitch the short edges of the end pieces together and press the seams open. With right sides facing and seams matching, stitch the end pieces around the ends of the main piece (diagram 1).

DIAGRAM 1

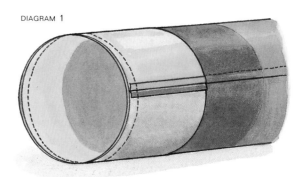

3 Open the end pieces. Press 1.5 cm (⅝ in) to the wrong side around the remaining edge of each end piece. Using a double thread, work a running stitch around the edge and pull up the thread to gather the ends in tightly (diagram 2). Finish the thread securely and stitch on a covered button at the center. Insert the bolster pad.

DIAGRAM 2

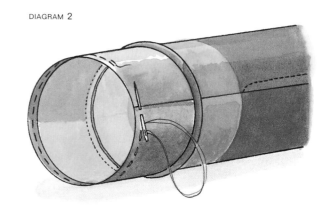

Plain-end bolster

Coordinating fabrics are used effectively on this smart bolster cover with plain round ends. The main section is cut in two pieces to combine the striped and patterned fabric and the ends are neatly piped in the striped fabric cut on the cross grain. There is a zipper opening in a seam at the back.

MATERIALS
2 coordinate upholstery fabrics
Sewing thread
Zipper about 7 cm (2³⁄₄ in) shorter than bolster pad
Piping cord
Bolster pad

CUTTING OUT

1.5 cm (⁵⁄₈ in) seam allowances are included unless instructions state otherwise.

Measure around the circumference of the bolster pad and along the pad's length. Divide up the length as desired between the two fabrics. Add on 3 cm (1¹⁄₄ in) to each measurement and cut the main pieces to this size. Cut two circular end pieces the same size as the end of the pad plus 1.5 cm (⁵⁄₈ in) all around.

1 With right sides facing, stitch the two fabrics together to make one main piece. Place the two lengthways edges of the main piece together with right sides facing and stitch for about 5 cm (2 in) at each end, leaving an opening at the center the length of the zipper teeth (diagram 1).

DIAGRAM 1

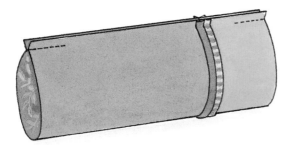

2 Stitch the zipper in place, taking care to keep the underlayer out of the way, see Zippers, page 25. Cover piping cord with bias strips of fabric and then stitch the piping around each end of the main piece, see Piping, page 18 (diagram 2).

DIAGRAM 2

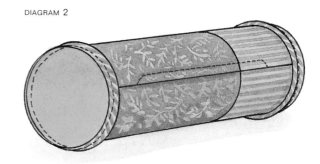

3 Divide each end of the main piece into four equal sections and mark with pins. In the same way, use pins to mark four equal sections around the edge of the circular end pieces. Leaving the zipper open, place the end pieces to the main piece with right sides facing, matching the pins. Pin together at these points (diagram 3).

DIAGRAM 3

4 Working from the circle side, pin the end pieces to the main piece between the marker pins, easing the fabric in to fit. It is advisable to tack the seams firmly. Stitch the seams as in Piping, page 18 (diagram 4). Turn right-side out through the zipper opening and insert the bolster pad.

DIAGRAM 4

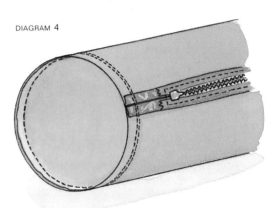

Seat pad with skirt

This style of seat pad has a flat skirt of fabric that protrudes over the chair seat around the front and side edges. It is fastened to the chair uprights with ties at the back. The seat area is padded with medium-weight wadding, but you could substitute 12 mm ($\frac{1}{2}$ in) foam for extra padding if you wish. If you are using a patterned fabric, arrange the pattern to run from the front to the back of the seat.

MATERIALS
Upholstery fabric
Sewing thread
Medium-weight wadding

CUTTING OUT

1.5 cm ($\frac{5}{8}$ in) seam allowances are included unless instructions state otherwise.

Measure the seat size, then add on 13 cm ($5\frac{1}{8}$ in) to the width and 8 cm ($3\frac{1}{4}$ in) to the depth from front to back. Cut out two pieces of fabric to these measurements. You may need to cut out a section at the back corners to accommodate the chair uprights. Cut four fabric ties 36 cm (14 in) by 5 cm (2 in).

1 Make four ties, see Ties, page 25. Place the ties onto the right side of the pad front, positioning them in pairs at each back corner so that they match the chair uprights. Arrange the ends of the ties level with the raw edge and stitch in place 1.5 cm ($\frac{5}{8}$ in) from the edge (diagram 1).

2 Place the back and front pad pieces together with right sides facing. Stitch the pieces together 1.5 cm ($\frac{5}{8}$ in) from the edges, beginning and finishing on the back edge 5 cm (2 in) in from the corners (diagram 2). Trim the corners, turn the pad right-side out, and press the seam at the edge.

DIAGRAM 1

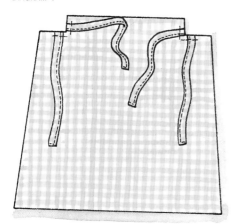

DIAGRAM 2

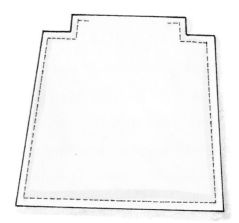

3 Beginning and finishing at the back edge, stitch around the sides and front edge of the pad, 5 cm (2 in) in from the edge, to form the skirt (diagram 3).

DIAGRAM 3

4 Cut the medium-weight wadding to the shape of the seat area of the pad. Slip the wadding in through the opening on the back edge. Tuck in the raw edges along the back edge and handstitch the opening closed (diagram 4).

DIAGRAM 4

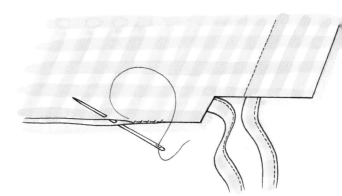

Patchwork seat pad

This version of the seat pad is made by joining fabric squares together to form a patchwork before cutting out the top. Stitch the patchwork squares along the side edges first to make three rows of three. Then stitch the rows together along their long edges. For a balanced design, number the fabrics and stitch them together in order 1 2 3 for the top row, 3 1 2 for the middle row and 2 3 1 for the base row.

MATERIALS
3 patchwork fabrics
Pattern paper
Fabric for pad back
Sewing thread
Medium-weight wadding

CUTTING OUT

1.5 cm ($^5/_8$ in) seam allowances are included unless instructions state otherwise.

Make a paper pattern to the size of your chair seat. Measure the longest distance, front to back or side to side, and divide this by three. Add 3 cm ($1^1/_4$ in) to this measurement and cut nine patchwork squares to that size. Cut four fabric ties 36 cm (14 in) by 5 cm (2 in).

1 Stitch the side edges of the top row of patchwork pieces together 1.5cm ($^5/_8$ in) in from the edge. Trim the seam allowances and press them open. Stitch the middle row and base row in the same way. In the same way stitch the rows together to make one piece, matching the seams carefully (diagram 1).

2 Place the paper pattern on the fabric. Add on 1.5 cm ($^5/_8$ in) seam allowance all around and cut out (diagram 2). Cut out the fabric for the pad back to the same size. Make four ties, see Ties, page 25, and then make up in the same way as the Seat pad with skirt, pages 42–44, but omitting the skirt stitching.

DIAGRAM 1

DIAGRAM 2

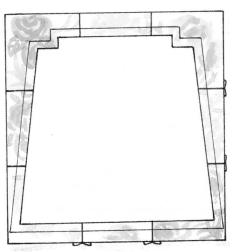

Box cushion

This piped cushion cover with a gusset can be used to re-cover an existing seat pad or fitted over a new foam pad. It has a zipper opening at the back of the gusset so that it can easily be removed for cleaning. Choose a zipper length about one third of the whole gusset length.

MATERIALS
Upholstery fabric
Sewing thread
Zipper, about one third of gusset length
Piping cord
Foam pad

NOTE
You can buy foam from specialist foam suppliers, who will cut it to size for you. Ask for advice on the most suitable type of foam and, if possible, choose a medium-density, flame-resistant type.

CUTTING OUT

1.5 cm (⅝ in) seam allowances are included unless instructions state otherwise.

Cut out a top and base piece to the size of the foam plus 1.5 cm (⅝ in) all around. Measure around the foam for the required finished gusset length. Cut the zipped section of the gusset the length of the zipper plus 5 cm (2 in) by the foam depth plus 6 cm (2¼ in). Then cut this section in half along its length. Cut the other section of the gusset the remainder of the length plus 3 cm (1¼ in) by the foam depth plus 3 cm (1¼ in).

1 With right sides facing and raw edges level, stitch two long edges of the zipper gussets together for 2.5 cm (1 in) at each end, leaving an opening the length of the zipper teeth at the center. Stitch the zipper into the opening, see Zippers, page 25 (diagram 1).

DIAGRAM 1

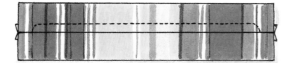

2 With right sides facing and raw edges level, stitch the short edges of the long gusset to the short edges of the zipper gusset. Press the seams open (diagram 2).

DIAGRAM 2

3 Stitch the piping around the edges of the top and the base pieces, see Piping, page 18.

4 Divide the edges of the top and base pieces into quarters and mark with pins (diagram 3). In the same way, mark both edges of the gusset into quarters.

DIAGRAM 3

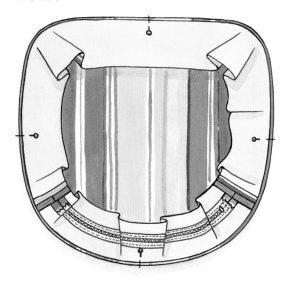

5 Open the zipper. Place the top edge of the gusset to the top piece with right sides facing and raw edges level. Match the marker pins and pin together at these points, then pin between the marks.

6 For a cover with rounded corners, make several snips close together into the gusset seam allowance at each curve – the tighter the curve, the closer the snips need to be (diagram 4). On a cushion cover with square corners, make a single snip into the gusset seam allowance at each corner so that the allowance will open out to fit around the corner (diagram 5). Tack, then stitch, the gusset in place. Stitch the base to the other edge of the gusset in the same way. Turn right-side out and press. Insert the foam pad.

DIAGRAM 4

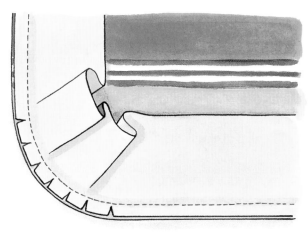

DIAGRAM 5

Variation

A box cushion can be made in almost any shape – just make sure that you make an accurate template of the seat area before you start.

Throw with mitered border

The double-mitred border on this throw looks as good on the back as on the front. This is a very useful method of trimming reversible fabric, giving it a fine, professional-looking finish.

CUTTING OUT

1.5 cm ($^5/_8$ in) seam allowances are included unless instructions state otherwise.

Cut the main fabric to the required size. Cut the borders 17 cm (6$^1/_2$ in) wide for a finished width of 7 cm (2$^3/_4$ in) by the length of the center panel plus twice the finished width of the border.

1 Stitch the borders following Double-mitred border, page 22, which also explains how to work out different sizes and border widths.

Throw edging variations

THROW WITH BEADED TRIM

A whole range of ready-made trims are now available – sew a double hem and then stitch on the beaded trim.

THROW WITH BLANKET STITCH

Blanket stitch is a simple hand-stitched edging for a throw, see Blanket stitch, page 13. On non-fray fabrics it can be worked directly over the edge, but even here a better finish is often achieved if a single hem to the depth of the stitching is folded to the wrong side first. This gives a firm edge and also gives a good line for keeping the stitching even. On fabrics that fray, such as velvet, fold a double hem before blanket stitching over it. Use a thick thread, such as wool, or a fine ribbon, as shown here.

THROW WITH FRINGED EDGE

Before you buy the fabric, check that it will fray neatly when the threads are pulled away. On closely woven fabric, the threads can just be pulled away to make a fringed edge. On loosely woven fabrics and for a more durable finish, stitch a line of narrow zigzag stitch in matching thread at the top of the fringe before fraying, see Fringing fabric, page 20.

THROW WITH BINDING

Binding gives a luxurious finish to a throw, especially if a fine satin or silk is used. If you cannot find silk or satin binding, make your own from ribbon or fabric. The double-binding method will give a very smart finish if a wide binding is preferred, see Double-binding method, page 17.

Tailored slip cover

This smart linen slipcover will give a new lease of life to a jaded dining room chair. It is made from natural linen with fine cream piping outlining the seat and the sides of the back. There are inverted pleats at the front corners of the skirt.

MATERIALS
Medium-weight upholstery fabric
Sewing thread
Piping cord
Contrasting fabric for piping

CUTTING OUT

1.5 cm ($^5/_8$ in) seam allowances are included unless instructions state otherwise.

Decide on the desired depth of the skirt. Beginning at the top of the chair seat, measure up the back of the chair back, across the top, down the front of the chair back and across the seat to the front edge, then add on the skirt depth plus 3 cm (1$^1/_4$ in). Measure across the back or seat, whichever is wider, add on 5 cm (2 in) and cut the main panel to this size. Measure the skirt around the two sides and front of the chair and add on 40 cm (16 in) for pleats and 5 cm (2 in) for side hem allowances. Cut the skirt to this length by the skirt depth plus 3 cm (1$^1/_4$ in).

1   Try the main piece on the chair, leaving the extra fabric allowed for the skirt depth, plus 1.5 cm ($^5/_8$ in) hem allowance, hanging down at the back. Pin down the sides of the chair back (diagram 1). Check the fit on both the back and seat and adjust if required, remembering to allow for seam allowances. Mark the top edge of the chair back, then unpin the fabric and remove from the chair.

DIAGRAM 1

2   Cover the piping cord with bias-cut strips, see Piping, page 18, to make sufficient to fit around the sides and front of the chair seat and up the side seams on the chair back. Starting at the top of the chair back, stitch piping to the front of the main piece down one side edge, around the chair seat and back up the other side edge, finishing the ends into the seam allowance (diagram 2).

DIAGRAM 2

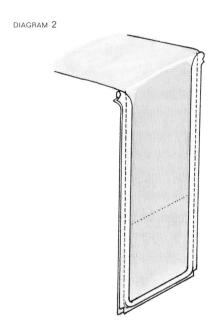

3 With right sides facing, stitch the front to the back down the side seams, leaving the skirt depth plus 1.5 cm (⅝ in) to hang free at the base of the back (diagram 3) .

DIAGRAM 3

4 With right sides facing, match the center of the seat front on the main panel with the center of the top edge of the skirt, then pin the skirt out to the front corners. At each corner, form a 10 cm (4 in) wide inverted pleat on the skirt, with its center at the corner, and snip into the seam allowance at the

center of the pleat (diagram 4). Continue pinning the skirt to the seat sides up to the back corners, leaving 2.5 cm (1 in) projecting beyond the back edges for the side hems. Tack, then stitch the skirt in place.

DIAGRAM 4

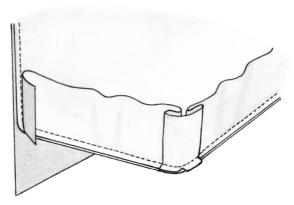

5 Zigzag stitch the lower edges of the skirt and back, and the remaining side edges of the skirt and back at the back corners. Press and stitch 1.5 cm (⅝ in) hems to the wrong side along the lower edges of the skirt and back. Press and stitch the hems to the wrong side down the remaining side edges of the skirt and back. Turn right-side out and press. Add a small bar stitch at the two front corners to hold the pleats neatly in place.

Simple slip cover

Surprisingly effective, the simple slip cover is basically just a rectangle of fabric, lined edge to edge, which drapes over the chair and fastens at the sides with fabric ties. A soft interlining is sandwiched between the fabric and lining to add a little luxury.

MATERIALS
Medium-weight upholstery fabric
Lining fabric
Soft interlining
Sewing thread

CUTTING OUT

1.5 cm (⅝ in) seam allowances are included unless instructions state otherwise.

Measure the area to be covered up the back of the chair, down the front, across the seat and down the front edge and add on 3 cm (1¼ in). Measure the width required at the widest point and add on 7 cm (2¾ in). Cut out the main fabric to these measurements. Cut eight ties 4 x 30 cm (1½ x 12 in).

1 Try the main piece on the chair. Check the fit on both the back and seat and adjust if required, remembering to allow for seams. Mark the positions for the ties on both the front and back with pins. Remove the fabric from the chair.

2 Cut the lining to the same size as the main fabric and the interlining 1.5 cm ($^5/_8$ in) smaller all around. Place the interlining to the wrong side of the main fabric. Press the edge of the main fabric over the edge of the interlining. Pin and tack the ties at the marked positions with their ends level with the raw fabric edge and the ties pointing outwards (diagram 1).

DIAGRAM 1

3 Place the lining to the main fabric with wrong sides facing. Tuck the raw edges of the lining under just inside the edge of the main fabric and stitch in place, catching in the ends of the ties (diagram 2).

DIAGRAM 2

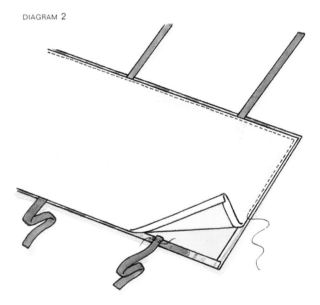

Tables

Square tablecloth

A classic square or rectangular tablecloth can protect a table top used for everyday or dress a table elegantly for a special meal. The square cloth shown here is finished with a deep hem for a classic look. The hem can be made on the wrong side of the fabric in the usual way for a plain look. If the fabric is reversible, you could make a feature of the hem by turning it onto the right side to give the effect of a mitered border. The finished hem is 4 cm (1½ in) deep, but you can make it narrower if you prefer.

MATERIALS
Cotton upholstery fabric
Sewing thread

CUTTING OUT
Cut out the cloth to the required size, adding 10 cm (4 in) to both the length and the width for the hem.

NOTE
Whenever possible, choose a fabric that is wide enough to make the tablecloth without seams. If seams are unavoidable, use a whole width of fabric for the center of the cloth and add half widths, or whatever is required, to each side. Join the pieces with a flat fell seam, see Seams, page 14.

1 Press 1 cm (³⁄₈ in), then 4 cm (1½ in) to the chosen side of the fabric to form the hem. Form and stitch miters at the corners, see Mitered hem, page 23 (diagram 1).

DIAGRAM 1

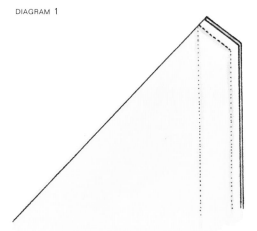

2 Refold the hem and press the corners. Pin, or tack in place if preferred, then stitch the hem along the inner fold (diagram 2).

DIAGRAM 2

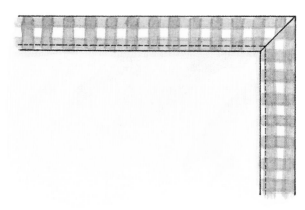

Tablecloth edging variations

TABLECLOTH WITH ORGANDY BORDER

You will need fabric, sewing thread and organdy for the border. Cut the cloth to required size. Cut the organdy borders 11 cm (4¼ in) wide, for a finished border width of 4 cm (1½ in), by the length of the cloth plus twice the finished border width. Make and stitch the borders as in Double-mitered border, page 22, trimming all the seam allowances to 5 mm (¼ in) as they are stitched.

TABLECLOTH WITH LACE EDGING

A lace edging will add a lovely touch to a plain white tablecloth. You can buy lace trims, such as broderie anglaise, in haberdasheries but it is worth looking out for old lace tablecloths in antique markets that you can recycle.

Stitch a double 1 cm (³⁄₈ in) hem around the table-cloth. Overlap the finished hem edge over the inner edge of the lace and stitch in place.

TABLECLOTH WITH ZIGZAG BORDER

You will need materials as for the basic square tablecloth plus contrasting pearl cotton or stranded cotton embroidery thread, an embroidery needle and matching sewing thread. Make the cloth as for the basic square tablecloth with the hem on the wrong side. Thread a long length of embroidery thread into the needle, bring it through to the front of the cloth from the wrong side and lay it along the hem, using the stitching as a guide. Using a close machine zigzag stitch, work over the embroidery thread to create a decorative border. Finish the ends of all the threads on the wrong side.

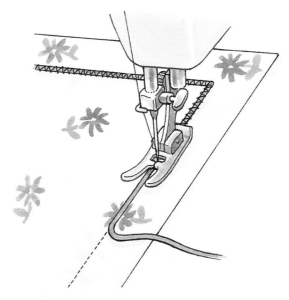

Circular tablecloth

Circular cloths are used to dress round dining tables and can be practical or luxurious depending on the fabric you choose. You can also make a feature of a small occasional table by making a circular cloth with a stylishly deep drop.

MATERIALS
Light-weight upholstery fabric
Sewing thread
Brown paper
String
Pencil

CUTTING OUT

1.5 cm ($^5/_8$ in) seam allowances are included unless instructions state otherwise.

Tie the pencil onto the end of the string. Measure and mark half the required diameter plus 1.5 cm ($^5/_8$ in) along the string from the pencil. Hold the marked string at one corner of the paper and, keeping the string taut, draw a quarter circle with the pencil (diagram 1).

Cut the paper along the drawn line. Fold the fabric into four, then place the straight edges of the pattern level with the folded edges of the fabric. Pin the paper in place and cut around the circular edge through all four layers of fabric.

NOTE

Because of the restriction of the fabric width, most circular tablecloths need to be joined. Use a full fabric width for a central panel and stitch more fabric to each side to make up the required width. Join the pieces before cutting out, using flat fell seams if the cloth is to be laundered frequently or plain seams if the cloth is mainly decorative, see Seams, page 14.

1 Open the fabric. Stitch around the circle 1.5 cm ($^5/_8$ in) in from the edge. Fold the raw edge over to the wrong side along the stitched line, pressing as you go. The stitching will naturally roll over to just inside the fold, giving a smooth curve.

2 Carefully turn under the raw edge to make a double hem. Press it as you go, easing in any fullness. Pin, tack, then stitch the hem in place (diagram 2).

DIAGRAM 2

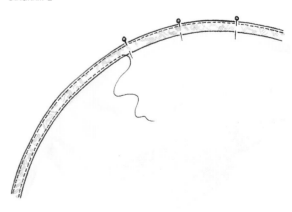

DIAGRAM 1

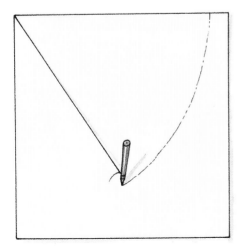

Beaded napkins

These pretty silk napkins with beaded trims are perfect for special occasions. The measurements given will make napkins with a generous finished size of 45 cm (17¾ in) square. If you prefer smaller napkins, cut the fabric 48 cm (19 in) square for a finished size of 40 cm (15¾ in).

MATERIALS
Silk fabric
Sewing thread
Small seed beads (optional)
Fine needle

CUTTING OUT
Cut out the fabric to 53 cm (21 in) square for each napkin.

1 Press 1 cm (⅜ in), then 3 cm (1¼ in) to the wrong side of the fabric to form the hem. Form and stitch miters at the corners, see Mitered hem, page 23 (diagram 1).

DIAGRAM 1

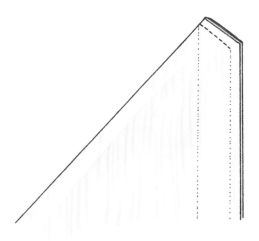

2 Stitch the hem in place. Using a fine needle, apply a row of small beads near the outer fold of the hem, spacing them about 3 cm (1¼ in) apart. Stitch each bead with two small backstitches before slipping the needle along inside the hem to the next bead position (diagram 2). Alternatively, stitch the beads in clusters of three along the center of the hem or in radiating lines at the corners.

DIAGRAM 2

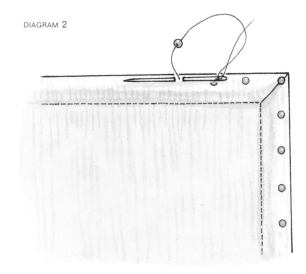

Napkin variations

CLASSIC LINEN NAPKIN

Cut out and make the napkin as in step 1 of the Beaded napkins, page 66, but fold the hem onto the right side of the fabric. Stitch the hem in place near its inner edge.

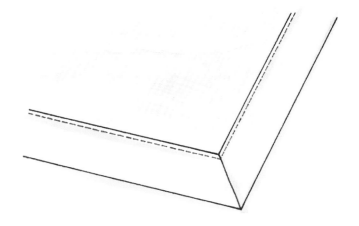

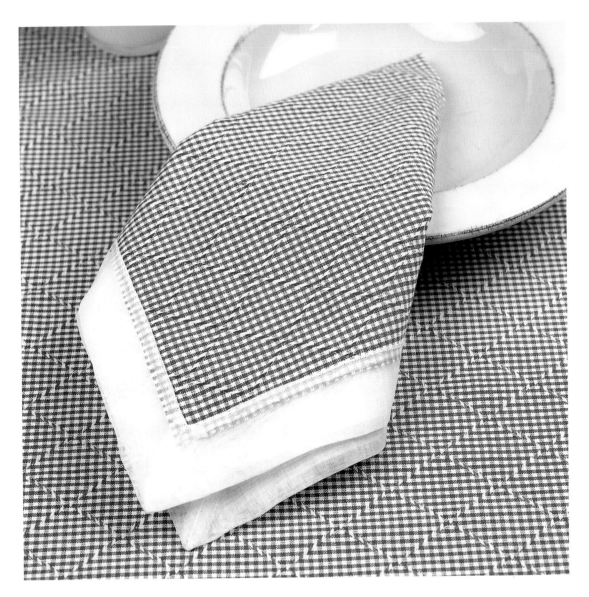

ORGANDY BORDER NAPKIN

Cut the napkin fabric 40 cm (15¾ in) square. Cut the organdy borders 9 cm (3½ in), for a finished width of 3 cm (1¼ in), by the length of the napkin fabric plus twice the finished border. Make and stitch the borders as in Double-mitered border, page 22, trimming all the seam allowances to 6 mm (¼ in) as they are stitched.

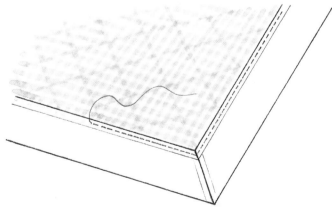

Silk table runner with tassel

This sumptuous silk table runner is lined edge to edge and is trimmed with a matching velvet ribbon. The points at each end are decorated with an elegant beaded tassel. The measurements given make a table runner with a finished size of 90 x 30 cm (35½ x 12 in).

MATERIALS
Silk fabric
Lining fabric
Pencil or marker
Ruler
Sewing thread
Velvet ribbon, 2 m (2¼ yds)
2 tassels

CUTTING OUT

1.5 cm (⅝ in) seam allowances are included unless instructions state otherwise.

Cut out a piece of fabric 93 x 33 cm (36½ x 13 in). Mark the center of each end with a pin. Measure 23 cm (9 in) in from each end along each side edge and mark with a pin. Draw lines between the central pins and the side pins. Cut the fabric along the marked lines to make the pointed ends (diagram 1). Mark and cut both ends of the lining in the same way.

DIAGRAM 1

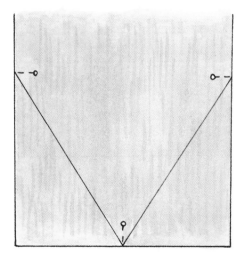

1 Place the lining and fabric right sides facing with raw edges level. Stitch together 1.5 cm (⅝ in) from the raw edges, leaving a 15 cm (6 in) opening on one long edge (diagram 2).

DIAGRAM 2

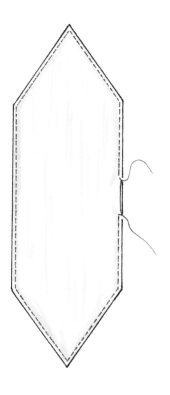

2   Trim the corners and turn the runner right-side out. Press the seam allowance to the inside along the opening and slip stitch the opening edges together. Pin and tack the velvet ribbon around the outer edge. Stitch the ribbon in place along both long edges. Stitch a tassel to the point at each end (diagram 3).

DIAGRAM 3

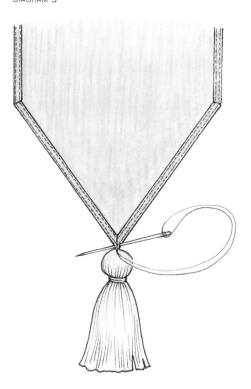

Table runner with organza border

The elegant oblong table runner has a fine linen center panel surrounded by a wide mitered border made from gold organza. The finished runner is 41 cm (16 in) wide.

MATERIALS
Linen fabric for center panel
Organza border fabric
Sewing thread

CUTTING OUT

1.5 cm (⅝ in) seam allowances are included unless instructions state otherwise.

Cut out two center panels 28 cm (11 in) wide by the required length minus 13 cm (5⅛ in). For the border, cut four strips 19 cm (7½ in) wide by the required length, see Double-mitered border, page 22.

1 Stitch the strips together to form a double-mitered border. Trim the miter seams to 5 mm ($^1/_4$ in) and press them open. Press the border with raw edges level and right sides out. With right sides facing, stitch both raw edges of the border together to the outer edge of the front center panel. Press the seam towards the center panel (diagram 1).

DIAGRAM 1

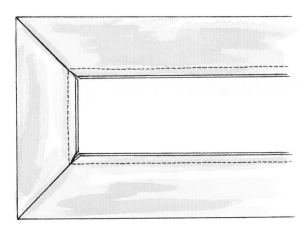

2 Press the seam allowance to the wrong side around the back center panel. Place this panel to the wrong side of the runner and stitch in place by hand along the line of the previous stitching (diagram 2).

DIAGRAM 2

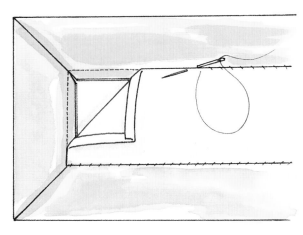

Beds

Buttoned pillowcase

The stylish buttoned pillowcases have deep hems on the two front panels which overlap and button together. The end panels are made in contrasting fabric to coordinate with the buttoned duvet cover on page 85.

MATERIALS
Cotton or poly-cotton sheeting
Sewing thread
3 buttons, 2 cm (³/₄ in) in diameter

NOTE
A standard American pillowcase measures
75 x 50 cm (30 x 20 in)

CUTTING OUT

1.5 cm (⁵/₈ in) seam allowances are included unless instructions state otherwise.

For the pillowcase back, measure the length and width of the pillow and add on 3 cm (1¹/₄ in) to each measurement. Cut out a piece of fabric to this size. Cut the front end panel to the same width and 35 cm (13³/₄ in) deep. Cut the main front panel the same width as the back and 2.5 cm (1 in) longer.

1 Press and stitch a double 7.5 cm (3 in) hem to the wrong side along one long edge of the front end panel and along one short edge of the main front panel (diagram 1).

DIAGRAM 1

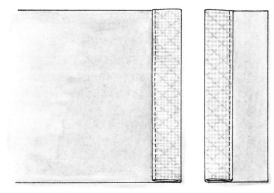

2 Mark three buttonhole positions centrally on the hem of the front end panel, placing one buttonhole at the center of the hem and one on either side, midway between the central one and the edge. Stitch the buttonholes at right angles to the edge (diagram 2).

DIAGRAM 2

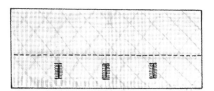

3 Place the front end panel to one end of the pillowcase back with right sides facing and raw edges level. Place the main front panel to the other end of the back in the same way, so that the hems overlap. Stitch the front panels to the back around all four edges (diagram 3).

DIAGRAM 3

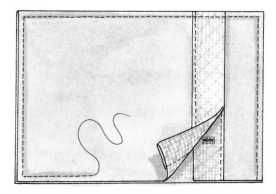

4 Trim the seam to 1 cm (³/₈ in) and zigzag stitch the edges together to prevent fraying. Turn the pillowcase right-side out and press the seam at the edge.

5 Stitch buttons to the main front panel hem to correspond with the buttonholes, placing the buttons to sit at the outer end of the buttonholes.

Housewife pillowcase

This simple, plain pillowcase is finished with a deep hem on the opening end and has a flap inside to hold the pillow in place.

MATERIALS
Cotton or poly-cotton fabric
Sewing thread

CUTTING OUT

1.5 cm (⁵⁄₈ in) seam allowances are included unless instructions state otherwise.

 Measure the length of the pillow, double this and add on 25 cm (10 in). Measure the width and add on 3 cm (1¹⁄₄ in). Cut out a piece of fabric to this size.

1   Press and stitch a double 1.5 cm (⁵⁄₈ in) hem across one short end. At the other short end press 1 cm (³⁄₈ in), then 5 cm (2 in) to the wrong side to make a deep hem and stitch in place.

2   With right sides facing, fold the end with the deep hem over so that it is 16 cm (6¹⁄₄ in) in from the edge with the narrow hem. Fold the projecting fabric back over the deep hem edge to form the flap (diagram 1).

DIAGRAM 1

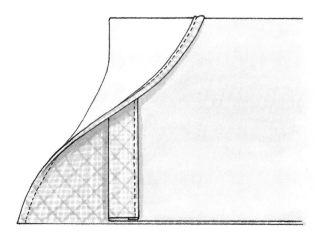

3   Stitch along both side edges, taking 1.5 cm (⁵⁄₈ in) seam allowances. Trim the seams to 1 cm (³⁄₈ in) and zigzag stitch the edges together to prevent fraying. Turn the pillowcase right side out and press.

Oxford pillowcase

This smart, tailored pillowcase has a generously wide 7 cm (2³⁄₄ in) border around the edge of the filled area. The inner edge of the border is trimmed with a row a decorative zigzag stitching worked over an embroidery thread.

MATERIALS
Cotton or poly-cotton fabric
Sewing thread
Stranded embroidery cotton or pearl cotton
embroidery thread

CUTTING OUT

1.5 cm (⁵⁄₈ in) seam allowances are included unless instructions state otherwise.

Measure the length of the pillow, double this and add on 50 cm (19³⁄₄ in). Measure the width of the pillow and add on 17 cm (6³⁄₄ in). Cut out a piece of fabric to this size.

1 Press and stitch a double 1.5 cm (⁵⁄₈ in) hem to the wrong side along each short edge.

2 With right sides together, fold one short edge over so that it is 33 cm (13 in) in from the other short edge. Fold the projecting short edge back over so that it overlaps the other short edge by 16 cm (6¹⁄₄ in)

(diagram 1). Stitch along both side edges, allowing for seams. Trim the seams to 1 cm (³⁄₈ in).

DIAGRAM 1

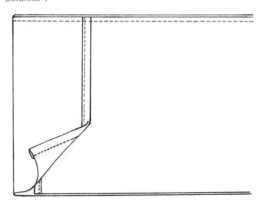

3 Turn the pillowcase right-side out and press the seams at the edges. Tack the overlapping flap to hold it in place. To create the border, stitch around the pillowcase 7 cm (2³⁄₄ in) in from the outer edges. For a more decorative finish, stitch around the pillowcase again using a machine zigzag stitch worked over a length of pearl cotton embroidery thread or all six strands of stranded embroidery cotton. Remove the tacking from the flap.

Basic duvet cover

This plain and simple duvet cover is easy to make and has an opening in
the hem across the base edge of the cover.

MATERIALS
Cotton or poly-cotton sheeting
Sewing thread
Press-stud tape

NOTE
Standard American duvet sizes are as follows:
165 x 210 cm (66 x 86 in) for a twin duvet and
200 x 225 cm (80 x 90 in) for a full duvet. Many
upholstery fabrics are wide enough for a twin
duvet cover, though they may not wash well and
often require a lot of ironing. Only custom-made
sheeting is wide enough for a full duvet cover and
has the advantage of an easy-care finish.

CUTTING OUT

1.5 cm ($^5/_8$ in) seam allowances are included unless
instructions state otherwise.

Measure the length and width of the duvet, add
11 cm (4$^1/_4$ in) to the length and 3 cm (1$^1/_4$ in) to the
width and cut out two pieces of fabric to this size.

1 Press and stitch a double 3 cm (1$^1/_4$ in) hem to the
wrong side along the lower edges of both pieces.

2 Place the two hemmed edges together with right
sides facing. Stitch the hemmed edges together just
inside the inner fold of the hem for 30 cm (12 in)
from each side, leaving an opening at the centre
(diagram 1).

DIAGRAM 1

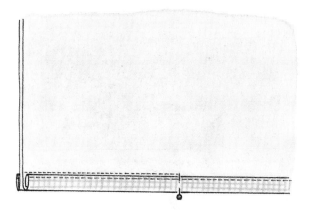

3 Cut the press-stud tape 5 cm (2 in) longer than the
opening, avoiding having a press stud near the ends.
Separate the two halves of the tape. Position one half
on one hem so that it projects beyond the opening
for 2.5 cm (1 in) at each end (diagram 2). Using a
zipper foot, stitch the tape in place along both its
long edges.

4 Fasten the second half of the tape to the first, then
pin it to the opposite hem – this ensures that the two
halves match exactly. Unfasten the tape and stitch
the second half in place in the same way as the first
(diagram 2).

DIAGRAM 2

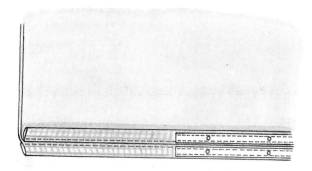

5 Fasten the tape. Stitch across the hems 2.5 cm (1 in) in from each end of the tape so the ends are enclosed.

6 With right sides facing and raw edges level, stitch the pieces together around the remaining three edges, taking a 1.5 cm ($^5/_8$ in) seam allowance. Trim the seams to 1 cm ($^3/_8$ in) and zigzag stitch the raw edges together (diagram 3). Turn the duvet cover right-side out and press the seams at the edges.

DIAGRAM 3

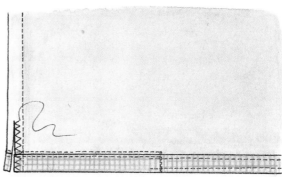

Duvet cover with flange

This version of the duvet cover has a generous 7 cm (2$^3/_4$ in) wide flange and will coordinate with the Oxford pillowcase, page 79. The duvet fills the inner pocket, which is sized to cover the duvet, leaving the flange flat at the edges.

MATERIALS
Cotton or poly-cotton sheeting
Sewing thread
Press-stud tape
Stranded embroidery cotton or pearl cotton embroidery thread

CUTTING OUT

1.5 cm ($^5/_8$ in) seam allowances are included unless instructions state otherwise.

Measure the length of the duvet, double this and add on 29 cm (11$^1/_2$ in). Measure the width of the duvet and add on 17 cm (6$^3/_4$ in). Cut out a piece of fabric to this size.

DIAGRAM 1

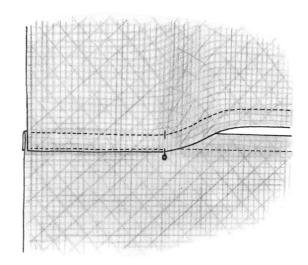

1 Press and stitch a double 3 cm (1$^1/_4$ in) hem to the wrong side along the two shorter edges.

2 With right sides facing up, lap one hemmed edge over the other. Stitch the hems together along the edge of the top hem for 30 cm (12 in) from each side, leaving an opening at the center (diagram 1).

3 Turn the cover through to the wrong side. Cut the press-stud tape 5 cm (2 in) longer than the opening, avoiding having a press stud near the ends. Separate the two halves of the tape. Position one half on one hem so that it projects beyond the opening for 2.5 cm (1 in) at each end. Using a zipper foot, stitch the tape in place along both its long edges.

4 Fasten the second half of the tape to the first and pin it to the opposite hemmed edge – this ensures that the two halves match exactly. Unfasten the tape and stitch the second half in place in the same way as the first (diagram 2).

DIAGRAM 2

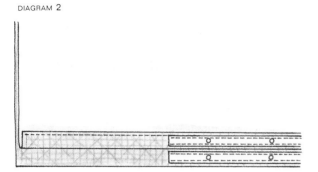

5 Fasten the tape and, working from the right side, stitch across the hems 2.5 cm (1 in) in from each end of the tape so the ends are enclosed (diagram 3).

DIAGRAM 3

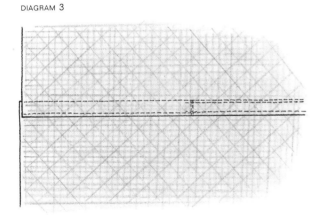

6 With right sides facing, arrange the fabric so the opening is at least 8.5 cm (3³⁄₈ in) from the lower fold edge and the raw edges are level at each side. Stitch together along both raw edges, taking 1.5 cm (⁵⁄₈ in) seam allowances (diagram 4).

DIAGRAM 4

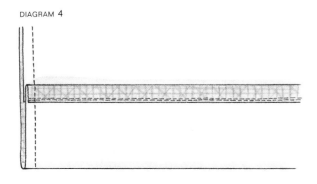

7 Trim the seams to 1 cm (³⁄₈ in). Turn the cover right-side out and press the seams at the edges. To form the flange, stitch around the side and lower edges 7 cm (2³⁄₄ in) in from the outer edge (diagram 5). To give a decorative finish, stitch around the flange again using a machine zigzag stitch worked over a length of pearl cotton embroidery thread or all six strands of stranded embroidery cotton (see page 63).

DIAGRAM 5

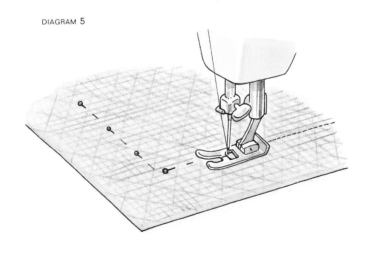

Duvet cover with border

Add a designer edge to the basic duvet cover with a crisp single mitred border stitched around a centre panel. The duvet fills the cover out to the edge of the border. Vary the look with different fabrics or combine co-ordinating checks and stripes for a country-style cover, taking care to match the pattern at the mitred corners.

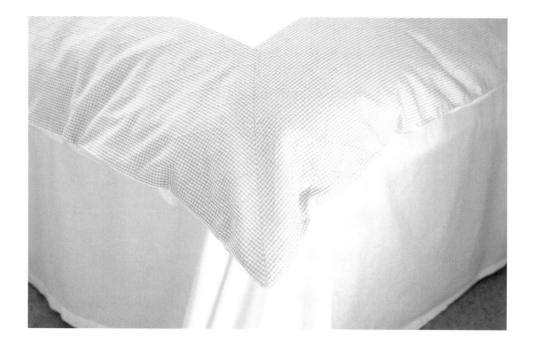

MATERIALS
Cotton or poly-cotton sheeting
Sewing thread
Press-stud tape

1 Cut a 26 cm (10¼ in) wide strip from the lower edge of the back piece. Press and stitch a double 3 cm (1¼ in) hem across both the cut edges. Overlap the hems and make the opening in the same way as the opening on the Duvet cover with flange, steps 2–5.

2 Stitch a mitered border around the front panel, see Single, mitered border, page 22. With right sides facing, stitch the duvet front to the back around the outer edges. Trim the seam allowances to 1 cm (³⁄₈ in) and zigzag stitch the raw edges together.

CUTTING OUT

1.5 cm (⁵⁄₈ in) seam allowances are included unless instructions state otherwise.

For the back of the cover, measure the length and width of the duvet, add 18 cm (7 in) to the length and 3 cm (1¼ in) to the width and cut out one piece of fabric to this size. For the front of the cover, subtract 37 cm (14½ in) from the measurements of the duvet and cut out the center panel to this size. For the border cut strips 23 cm (9 in) wide by the required length, see Single-mitered border, page 22.

Buttoned duvet cover

The smart buttoned duvet cover has a wide contrast band across its top edge which buttons onto the main front panel to form the opening. The cover is designed to coordinate with the buttoned pillowcase on page 76.

MATERIALS
Cotton or poly-cotton sheeting
Sewing thread
Buttons, 2 cm (³⁄₄ in) in diameter

CUTTING OUT

1.5 cm (⁵⁄₈ in) seam allowances are included unless instructions state otherwise.

For the back of the duvet cover, measure the length and width of the duvet and add on 3 cm (1¹⁄₄ in) to each measurement. Cut out a piece of fabric to this size. Cut the top front panel to the same width by 46 cm (18 in) deep. Cut the lower front panel the same width by the length of the back minus 8.5 cm (3³⁄₈ in).

1 Press and stitch a double 7.5 cm (3 in) hem to the wrong side across the lower edge of the top front panel. Repeat across the top edge of the lower front panel.

2 Stitch a row of 2.5 cm (1 in) long vertical buttonholes centrally along the top panel hem, spacing them about 30 cm (12 in) apart.

3 Place the top panel to the top edge of the back piece with right sides facing and raw edges level. Place the lower front panel to the lower edge of the back in the same way, so that its hem overlaps the hem on the top panel.

4 Stitch together around all four edges, 1.5 cm (⁵⁄₈ in) in from the raw edges. Trim the seam to 1 cm (³⁄₈ in) and zigzag stitch the raw edges together to prevent fraying.

5 Turn the cover right-side out and press the seam at the edge. Stitch the buttons onto the hem of the lower front panel to match the buttonhole positions, placing the buttons to sit at the lower edge of the buttonholes.

Throwover bedcover

This, the simplest of all bedcovers, is just a rectangle of fabric hemmed around the edges. When measuring, remember to make an allowance for the cover to fit up and over the pillows.

MATERIALS
Heavyweight upholstery fabric, such as cotton matelassé
Sewing thread

CUTTING OUT

Measure the width of the bed and add on two drops to the floor plus 8 cm (3¼ in) for the hem. Measure the length of the bed and add on one drop to the floor plus 8 cm (3¼ in) for hems, remembering to add an allowance to fit over the pillows. If the fabric needs to be joined, add on 4 cm (1½ in) for each seam. Cut out the fabric to these measurements (diagram 1).

DIAGRAM 1

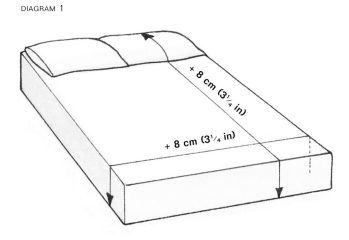

1 If the fabric is not wide enough to cut the whole required width of the bedcover as one piece, use the full width of the fabric to make a central panel and add the extra fabric required to either side. Stitch the panels together with 2 cm (¾ in) seams, place the raw edges together and press the seams away from the central panel (diagram 2).

DIAGRAM 2

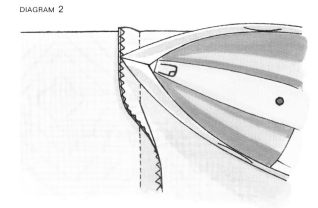

2 Press 1 cm (⅜ in), then 3 cm (1¼ in) hems to the wrong side along the side edges. Stitch the hems in place. Then press and stitch double hems along the top and bottom edges in the same way (diagram 3).

DIAGRAM 3

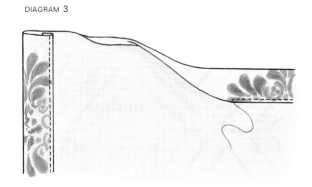

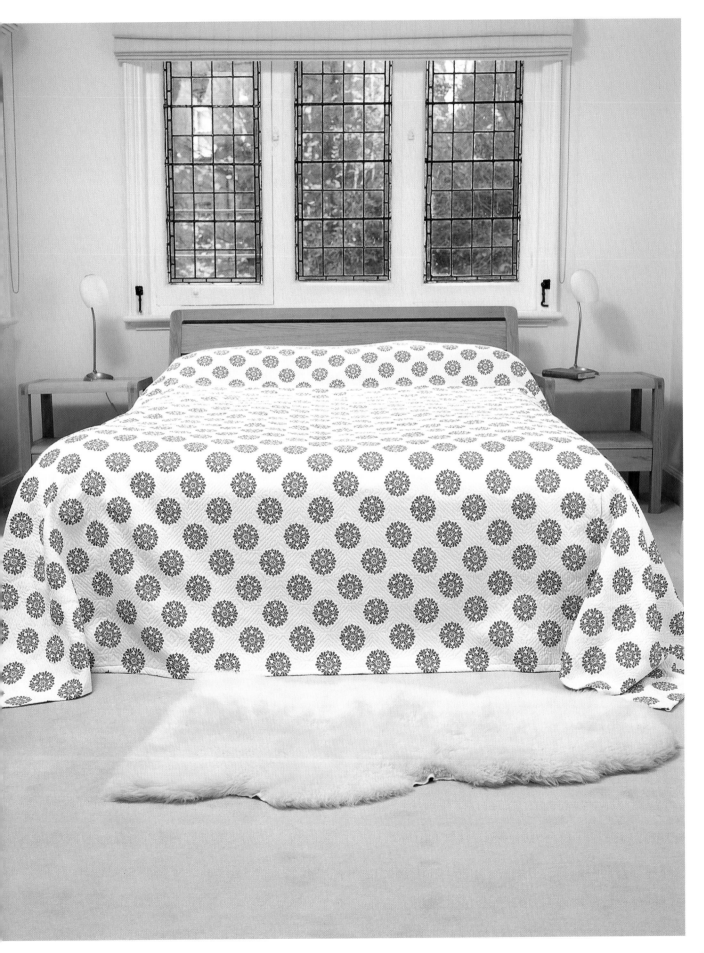

Throwover bedcover with curved corners

This is almost identical to the throwover bedcover on page 86, except that the corners are curved for a slightly more finished look.

MATERIALS
Heavyweight upholstery fabric, such as
cotton matelassé
Sewing thread
Marker pen and string
Cotton fabric for binding

CUTTING OUT

Measure and cut out the fabric as for the Throwover bedcover, page 86, omitting the 8 cm (3¼ in) allowed for hems. If required, join fabric pieces as for the Throwover bedcover, step 1.

1 Mark the curved corners as follows. Measure along the fabric edges 30 cm (12 in) from either side of the first base corner and mark with pins. Place another pin equidistant from these two pins, so that the three pins and the base corner form a square. Tie the marker pen onto the string and mark the string 30 cm (12 in) away from the pen. Position the marked end of the string on the inner corner of the square. Holding the string taut, draw a curved line between the two outer pins with the pen. Trim the base corner along the curved line (diagram 1). Repeat for the second base corner.

DIAGRAM 1

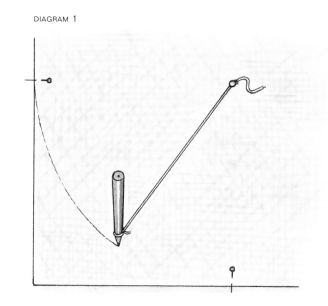

2   Cut and join bias strips to fit around the two sides,
    curved corners and lower edge, see Bias binding,
    page 16. Cut and join another strip to fit across the
    top edge plus 2 cm (³⁄₄ in). Make into binding and
    bind the side and lower edges, see Binding an edge,
    page 16, easing the binding to fit around the curves
    (diagram 2).

DIAGRAM 2

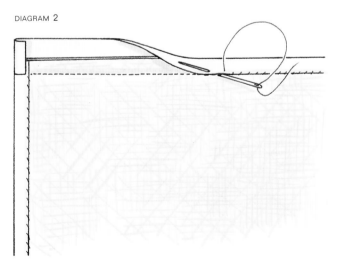

3   With right sides facing, stitch the binding to the top
    edge, allowing 1 cm (³⁄₈ in) to project at each end.
    Fold the projecting ends onto the wrong side of the
    binding. Turn the binding over to the wrong side and
    handstitch the second edge in place.

Fitted bedcover

This smart, fitted cover has a straight skirt with inverted pleats. Neat piping inserted in the seam gives the edge of the main panel a crisp outline.

MATERIALS
Medium-weight upholstery fabric
Sewing thread
Piping cord

CUTTING OUT

1.5 cm ($^5/_8$ in) seam allowances are included unless instructions state otherwise.

Cut out the main panel to the required finished width plus 3 cm ($1^1/_4$ in) by the required finished length, remembering to add an allowance to fit over the pillows, plus 5.5 cm ($2^1/_8$ in). Allow extra for any seams. Cut the skirt to the required finished depth plus 5.5 cm ($2^1/_8$ in). For the skirt length, double the required finished length of the main panel, plus its width, plus 20 cm (8 in) for each pleat and 8 cm ($3^1/_4$ in) for hems. Plan the pleats so one is positioned at each corner. Allow extra for seams.

1   If required, join the fabric to make up the width of the main panel, using the full width of fabric for a central panel and adding narrower widths at either side. Drawing around a saucer, mark curves at the two lower corners to match the mattress shape and trim the fabric.

2   On the skirt allow 4 cm ($1^1/_2$ in) for the side hem, then measure the distance to the first pleat, i.e., 30 cm (12 in) for the bedcover shown here, and mark with a pin. Measure along another 10 cm (4 in) and mark with a pin, then a further 10 cm (4 in) and mark with a pin. Bring the two outer pins over to meet at the central pin to form an inverted pleat, see Inverted

pleats, page 26. Pin and tack the pleat in place across the top edge. Measure the required distance to the next pleat, i.e., 25 cm (10 in), then mark and form the pleat in the same way.

3   Continue joining fabric where required at the back fold of the pleats until all pleats are tacked. The distance, including hem allowance, between the last pleat and the edge of the skirt should be the same as at the beginning (34 cm/$13^1/_2$ in). Stitch around the top edge to hold the pleats in place (diagram 1).

DIAGRAM 1

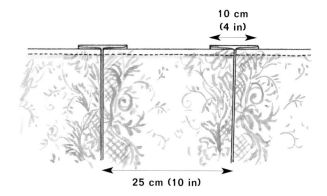

10 cm (4 in)

25 cm (10 in)

4   Cover the piping cord, see Piping, page 18. Beginning and finishing 4 cm ($1^1/_2$ in) in from the top edge, stitch the piping around the sides and lower edge of the main panel, snipping into the edge of the piping to fit around the curved corners.

5   Place the top edge of the skirt onto the piped edge of the main panel with right sides facing and raw edges level. Match and pin the ends of the skirt to the top corners of the panel and the corner pleats to the center of the curved corners. Then pin the edges together between these points and tack (diagram 2). Stitch in place with the main panel uppermost.

DIAGRAM 2

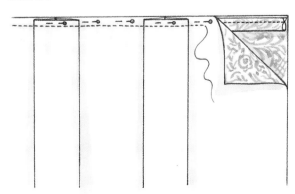

6 Press 1 cm (³⁄₈ in), then 3 cm (1¹⁄₄ in) to the wrong
side to form a hem around the lower edge of the skirt
and stitch in place. Press and stitch a hem across the
ends of the skirt and top of the main panel in the
same way. Form the pleats along the length of the
skirt and press in place.

Patchwork quilt

A patchwork quilt is an eye-catching feature in a bedroom and this version, with its big, bold squares, does not take long to make. Three squares across by five down make a quilt with a finished size of 100 x 150 cm (39 x 59 in). Each square has a finished size of 25 cm (10 in) and the border is 12.5 cm (5 in) wide.

MATERIALS
Selection of cotton fabrics for patchwork
Sewing thread
110 g (4 oz) wadding
Cotton backing fabric

CUTTING OUT

1.5 cm (⅝ in) seam allowances are included unless instructions state otherwise.

Cut out as many 28 cm (11 in) patchwork squares as required. Cut the strips for the mitered border 15.5 cm (6 in) wide by the length and width of the finished patchwork plus 25 cm (10 in). Cut the wadding and backing fabric to the size of the finished patchwork with mitered border attached.

1 Arrange the patchwork pieces as required. With right sides facing and raw edges level, pin and stitch a horizontal row of squares together along their side edges. Stitch the remaining squares into horizontal rows in the same way and press the seams open (diagram 1).

DIAGRAM 1

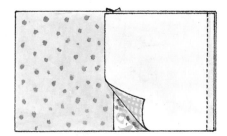

2 With right sides facing, place the top of one row to the base of the row above it, pinning the seams together before stitching so that they match exactly. Stitch all the rows together in this way and press the seams open (diagram 2).

DIAGRAM 2

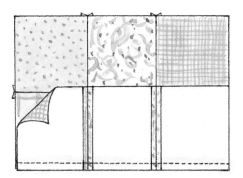

3   Pin on the borders, matching the center of the border to the center of the patchwork edge and working outwards towards the corners. Stitch the borders in place and mitere the corners, see Single-mitered border, page 22. Press the border seams open (diagram 3).

DIAGRAM 3

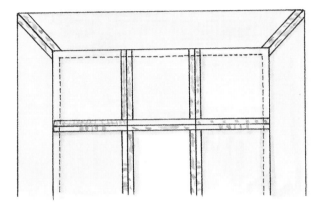

4   Place the wadding to the wrong side of the quilt and trim to fit. If the wadding needs to be joined, butt the edges together and stitch with a large, loose herring-bone stitch, see Herringbone stitch, page 13. Pin and tack around the edge. With right sides facing, pin and tack the backing fabric to the right side of the quilt. Stitch together around the outer edges (diagram 4), leaving a 20 cm (8 in) gap to turn through. Trim the excess wadding from the seam-allowance. Trim the corners, turn the quilt right side out and arrange the seam neatly at the edge. Tuck in the seam allowances along the opening and stitch it closed by hand.

DIAGRAM 4

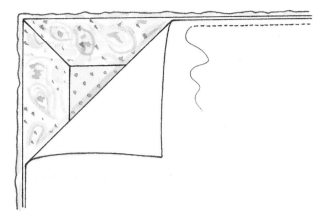

5   Arrange the three layers of the patchwork quilt evenly, smoothing the fabric flat on both sides. Pin through the layers along the outer patchwork seam, then along the lines of the patchwork squares. Tack, then machine stitch along the horizontal and vertical seams (diagram 5).

DIAGRAM 5

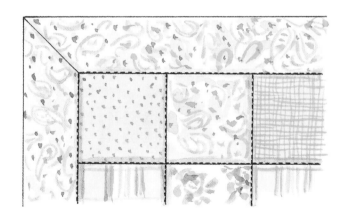

Gathered valance

A valance fits over the base of the bed underneath the mattress with a skirt that hangs to the floor to hide the bed base. Fabric with a ready-made scalloped edge gives a pretty finish to the lower edge. If you use a plain fabric for the skirt, finish the edge with a hem.

MATERIALS
Cotton or poly-cotton sheeting fabric
Inexpensive fabric or old sheet (optional)
Sewing thread

CUTTING OUT
1.5 cm (⁵⁄₈ in) seam allowances are included unless instructions state otherwise.

For the bed panel, measure the length of the mattress and add on 3.5 cm (1³⁄₈ in), then measure the width and add on 3 cm (1¹⁄₄ in). For a bed panel with a border, see Note below, cut out the central section from inexpensive fabric and cut 10 cm (4 in) wide borders from the skirt fabric to fit around its side and base edges to make up the required size. For the skirt depth, measure from the top of the bed base to the floor and add on 6.5 cm (2¹⁄₄ in) for a hemmed lower edge, or 1.5 cm (⁵⁄₈ in) if using fabric with a ready-made scalloped edge. For the skirt length, add the bed width to twice its length and double that measurement.

NOTE
For economy, you can cut the central area of the bed panel, which will not be seen, from an old sheet or inexpensive fabric, adding a narrow border of the skirt fabric around the edge where it might show. If you prefer to use sheeting, you can cut the whole bed panel as one piece.

1 If required, make up the size of the bed panel by joining the borders to the edges of the central section with narrow seams, see Seams and hems, page 14. Drawing around a saucer, mark curves at the two lower corners of the bed panel and trim to shape (diagram 1).

DIAGRAM 1

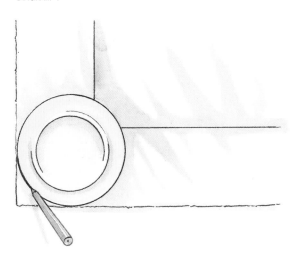

2 Cut as many fabric widths as required to make up the skirt length. Join the skirt pieces with narrow seams. If required, press a double 2.5 cm (1 in) hem to the wrong side around the lower edge of the skirt and stitch in place.

3 Measure the side and base edges of the bed panel and divide into six equal lengths. Mark with pins. Divide the top edge of the skirt into six equal lengths and mark with pins in the same way. Gather the top edge of the skirt, stopping and restarting at the pins (diagram 2). Stitch the skirt to the bed panel, matching the marked points, see Frills, page 21.

DIAGRAM 2

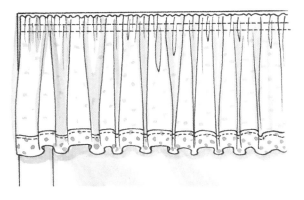

4 Press a double 1 cm ($\frac{3}{8}$ in) hem to the wrong side along the side edges of the skirt and across the top edge of the bed panel (diagram 3).

DIAGRAM 3

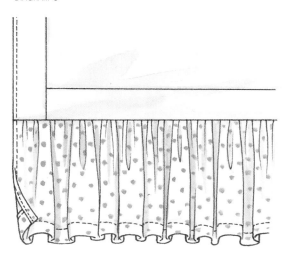

Fitted valance

The fitted valance is plain along the side and base edges with inverted pleats at the corners for a smart tailored look. This valance is made with square corners to emphasise the sharp lines.

MATERIALS
Cotton or poly-cotton sheeting
Sewing thread

CUTTING OUT

1.5 cm ($\frac{5}{8}$ in) seam allowances are included unless instructions state otherwise.

For the bed panel, measure the length of the mattress and add on 3.5 cm ($1\frac{3}{8}$ in), then measure the width and add on 3 cm ($1\frac{1}{4}$ in). For the skirt depth, measure from the top of the bed base to the floor and add on 6.5 cm ($2\frac{1}{2}$ in). For the skirt length, add the bed width to twice its length and add on 84 cm (33 in).

If you wish to make the central section of the bed panel from inexpensive fabric, cut out the fabric and add borders as for the Gathered valance, page 96.

1 If required, make up the size of the bed panel by joining the borders to the edges of the central section with narrow seams, see Seams and hems, page 14.

2 Cut as many fabric widths as required to make up the skirt length. Join the skirt pieces with narrow seams. Press a double 2.5 cm (1 in) hem to the wrong side around the lower edge of the skirt and stitch in place.

3 Measure the length of the side edge of the bed panel minus 1.5 cm ($^5/_8$ in) along the top edge of the skirt. Mark with a pin. Measure along a further 20 cm (8 in) and then another 20 cm (8 in) and mark with pins. Bring the outer pins over to meet at the central pin to form an inverted pleat. Tack the pleat in place along the top edge (diagram 1). Measuring from the other end of the skirt, make another pleat in the same way, see Pleats, page 26.

4 With right sides facing and raw edges level, pin the skirt around the side and base edges of the bed panel, checking that the pleats align with the lower corners. Snip the fabric at the center of the pleats so that it fits around the corners. Tack and stitch in place.

5 Press a double 1 cm ($^3/_8$ in) hem to the wrong side along the side edges of the skirt and across the top edge of the bed panel. Stitch in place.

DIAGRAM 1

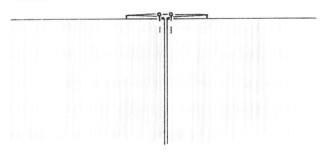

Headboard

The pretty padded cover simply folds over the headboard and ties at the sides. The narrow stripes have a clean, country look and add charm and coordination to a fresh color scheme. By replacing the lining with a contrasting fabric, you can make the headboard reversible too.

MATERIALS
Cotton upholstery fabric
Sewing thread
100 g (4 oz) wadding
Lining fabric

CUTTING OUT

1.5 cm ($^5/_8$ in) seam allowances are included unless instructions state otherwise.

Measure the width of the headboard and add 7 cm ($2^3/_4$ in). Measure the required depth, double this and add on the thickness of the headboard plus 3 cm ($1^1/_4$ in). Cut out the main fabric, wadding and lining fabric to the established measurements. Cut out four ties 43 x 4 cm (17 x $1^1/_2$ in).

1 Make the ties, see Ties, page 25. Fold the main fabric in half with right sides outside. Mark the positions for the ties at the side edges of both fabric layers, placing the top pair 15 cm (6 in) down from the fold and the lower pair 17 cm ($6^3/_4$ in) up from the lower edge. Adjust the position for the ties if desired. Unfold the fabric and tack the ties to the marked positions on the right side of the fabric with their raw ends level with the raw edges of the fabric (diagram 1).

DIAGRAM 1

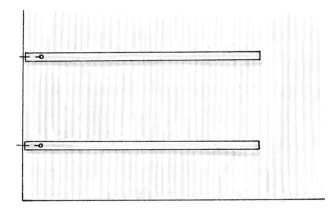

2 Place the wadding to the wrong side of the fabric and tack around the edge. With right sides facing, pin and stitch the lining to the fabric around all edges, leaving a 30 cm (12 in) opening at the center of the back lower edge (diagram 2).

DIAGRAM 2

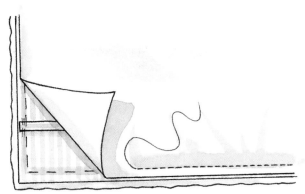

3 Trim the wadding from the seam allowances. Turn the headboard right-side out through the opening. Lightly press the seam at the edge. Press in the raw edges along the opening and slipstitch the opening closed.

Canopy

A pretty draped canopy will add lots of style to a simple day bed. The fabric is held in place by means of stitched-on casings that are slipped over wooden rods attached to the wall with brackets.

MATERIALS
Lightweight upholstery fabric
Sewing thread
3 wooden rods
3 brackets

NOTE
Choose a fairly light-weight fabric that drapes well and allow plenty of fullness. The width of the light-weight linen illustrated is about 2½ times the length of the rods; if you use a thicker fabric, you could reduce the fullness. Using the full width of fabric avoids the need for hems at the front and back edges.

1 Cut the wooden rods to the required length; the rods illustrated are 54 cm (21¼ in) long for 140 cm (55 in) wide fabric. Paint the rods white if you wish. Fix the rods to the top of the brackets and fix the brackets to the wall at the required positions. The center rod shown here is 2 m (78 in) up from the floor and the side rods are 30 cm (12 in) lower.

2 Drape the fabric over the rods to establish the required length and mark the positions for the casings on the fabric at each rod. Cut the fabric to the required length and stitch a close zigzag stitch across each end to neaten.

3 Cut three casing strips wide enough to accommodate the rod and bracket plus 2 cm (¾ in). Press 1 cm (⅜ in) to the wrong side along the long edges of each casing. Place the casings to the wrong side of the fabric across its width at the positions marked for the rods. Stitch in place along both long edges and the front edge.

4 Press the canopy, then, starting at the back edge, thread each casing onto its appropriate rod and bracket. Arrange the fullness evenly.

Windows

Unlined tab top curtains

The top edge of these simple unlined curtains is finished with fabric tabs so that you can hang them from a curtain pole.

MATERIALS
Lightweight curtain fabric
Sewing thread

CUTTING OUT

1.5 cm (⁵⁄₈ in) seam allowances are included unless the instructions state otherwise.

Decide how full you want the curtains to be. Unless a window is extremely narrow, you will need to join widths of fabric to get the required curtain width. Work out the required curtain width and add on 10 cm (4 in). Measure the required length and add on 17.5 cm (7 in). Cut the tabs twice the required width plus 3 cm (1¼ in) by 22 cm (8¾ in) long. Cut an 8 cm (3¼ in) deep facing to the required curtain width plus 3 cm (1¼ in).

NOTE

The width and length of the tabs can be adjusted to suit the fabric and the size of the pole. A heavy fabric hung from a thick pole will require larger tabs than a fine fabric hung from a thin pole. Tabs that are cut 10 cm (4 in) wide will have a finished width of 3.5 cm (1³⁄₈ in) and are suitable for lightweight or medium-weight fabrics.

1 Join any fabric widths if required with plain seams pressed open. Press 2.5 cm (1 in) double hems to the wrong side along the side edges of the curtain and stitch in place.

2 Fold the tabs in half lengthways with right sides facing and stitch the two raw edges together. Trim the seam and press it open. Turn the tabs right-side out and press the seam to one edge (diagram 1).

DIAGRAM 1

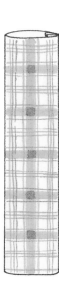

3 Fold each tab in half widthways and pin it, pointing downwards, to the right side of the curtain with its raw edges level with the top edge of the curtain. Place a tab at each side edge and arrange the others evenly in between, about 12–15 cm (4¾–6 in) apart. Pin and tack the tabs in place (diagram 2).

DIAGRAM 2

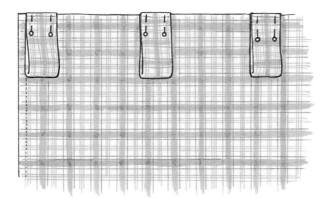

4 With right sides facing and top raw edges level, place the facing across the curtain on top of the tabs, allowing it to project for 1.5 cm (⅝ in) at each end. Stitch in place across the top edge (diagram 3).

DIAGRAM 3

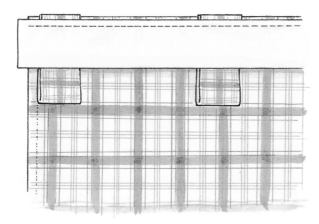

5 Press the facing over to the wrong side. If your chosen fabric is translucent, trim the fabric seam allowances to 1 cm (⅜ in). Press the seam allowances to the wrong side of the fabric along both sides and across the lower edge of the facing. Stitch the facing to the curtain along the pressed edges. Topstitch across the top edge of the facing (diagram 4).

DIAGRAM 4

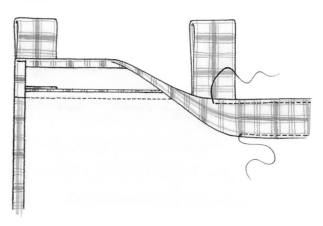

6 Press an 8 cm (3¼ in) deep double hem to the wrong side across the lower edge of the curtain and stitch in place.

Variation

This curtain, using very sheer, embroidered fabric, is particularly effective and looks lovely when the light shines through the fabric.

Unlined curtain with fold-over top

On this pretty curtain, a section of the fabric at the top is simply folded over and attached to clip-on hooks to hang from curtain rings. Stitched tucks, which show up well against the light, are worked across the curtain on the fold-over section and above the base hem. Choose a reversible fabric, as the back of the fabric forms the front of the fold-over.

MATERIALS
Reversible sheer curtain fabric
Sewing thread
Curtain clips

CUTTING OUT

1.5 cm ($\frac{5}{8}$ in) seam allowances are included unless instructions state otherwise.

Decide how full you want the curtain to be and measure the required width. Add on 4 cm (1$\frac{1}{2}$ in) if side hems are required; alternatively, use the fabric selvedges as the side edges. Measure the required length and add on the depth of the fold-over, plus 20 cm (8 in) for hems and 15 cm (6 in) for tucks.

1 If side hems are required, press 1 cm ($\frac{3}{8}$ in) double hems to the wrong side along the two side edges of the curtain and stitch in place.

2 At the top edge, press the depth of the fold-over section plus 14 cm (5$\frac{1}{2}$ in) for the tucks and hem over onto the right side. At the lower edge of the fold-over, press a double 4 cm (1$\frac{1}{2}$ in) hem to the wrong side and stitch in place. On the right side of the fold-over, fold and press a crease 4.5 cm (1$\frac{3}{4}$ in) up from the top of the hem. Stitch 1.5 cm ($\frac{5}{8}$ in) in from the crease to form a tuck, see Tucks, page 27 (diagram 1).

3 Press the tuck downwards. Press a second crease 4.5 cm (1$\frac{3}{4}$ in) above the previous tuck stitching and stitch a second tuck 1.5 cm ($\frac{5}{8}$ in) in from the crease.

4 On the main part of the curtain, fold a double 6 cm (2$\frac{1}{4}$ in) hem to the wrong side across the lower edge and stitch. Make three tucks above the hem in the same way as the previous tucks (diagram 2). Clip on curtain clips at regular intervals along the top of the curtain.

DIAGRAM 1

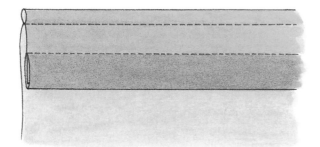

DIAGRAM 2

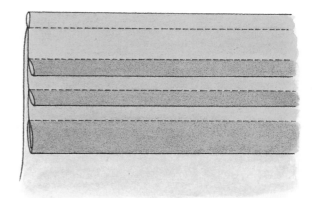

Unlined curtain panel

A patchwork of fine lawn panels creates a vibrant mosaic effect on this translucent curtain. It has a simple fold-over casing at the top, so that it can be threaded onto a tension rod or wooden doweling. A separate casing at the lower edge holds a length of doweling to add weight to the curtain.

MATERIALS
Lawn fabrics
Sewing thread
Ribbons for trimming
Wooden doweling

CUTTING OUT

Cut out as many fabric panels of varying sizes as required, allowing 1 cm ($^3/_8$ in) for seams for joining the pieces, 2 cm ($^3/_4$ in) for the side hems, and 3.5 cm ($1^3/_8$ in) for the top casing. For the lower casing, cut a strip 12 cm ($4^3/_4$ in) deep by the required width of the curtain panel.

1 Lay out the lawn panels in vertical rows – each panel within a row should have the same width. Join the lawn panels widthways with 1 cm ($^3/_8$ in) seams to make vertical panels. If you wish, stitch ribbon trims along selected seams. Then join the panels length-ways with 1 cm ($^3/_8$ in) seams to make the whole curtain panel, adding ribbon trims if required.

2 To make a window patch, take a smaller rectangle of lawn, press the raw edges under and stitch the piece onto a lawn panel. Trim away the fabric behind the patch. Neaten the raw edges at the back with machine zigzag stitch (diagram 1).

3 Stitch double 1 cm ($^3/_8$ in) hems to the wrong side along the side edges of the curtain and lower casing. Press 1 cm ($^3/_8$ in), then 2.5 cm (1 in) to the wrong side across the top edge and stitch to make a casing. Fold the lower casing in half with the right sides outside. Stitch the casing to the lower edge with right sides facing and raw edges level, then press the casing downwards (diagram 2).

DIAGRAM **1**

DIAGRAM **2**

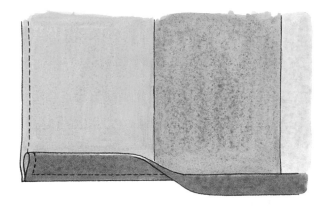

Tube-lined curtains

Tube-lined curtains are the easiest type of lined curtain to make. The lining is cut narrower than the fabric, and the side edges of the lining and curtain are simply sewn together. The narrower lining pulls the fabric over to the wrong side to give the effect of a hem. However, these hems will have to be realigned and re-pressed each time the curtain is laundered.

CALCULATING FABRIC AMOUNTS FOR CURTAINS

For the curtain width, multiply the width of the curtain track or pole by the amount of fullness required by the heading tape – this is usually 2–2$\frac{1}{2}$ times the track or pole length. Add on allowances for side hems and seams as given for each project. Then, if necessary, round up the amount to the next full width or half width. For the length, add on allowances for the top hem and lower hem as given for each project. Multiply the length required by the number of widths to give the fabric amount. If the fabric has a pattern that needs to be matched, you will need to allow for it on each fabric width or half width.

MATERIALS
Curtain fabric
Sewing thread
Lining fabric
Heading tape

CUTTING OUT

1.5 cm ($\frac{5}{8}$ in) seam allowances are included unless instructions state otherwise.

Calculate the fabric amounts (see left). For the width, allow 4 cm (1$\frac{1}{2}$ in) for each side hem and 3 cm (1$\frac{1}{4}$ in) for each seam. For the length, add on 4 cm (1$\frac{1}{2}$ in) for the top hem and 15 cm (6 in) for the lower hem. If the curtains are long, you may wish to make a deeper hem.

Cut the lining 4 cm (1$\frac{1}{2}$ in) shorter than the curtain fabric at the top edge and 10 cm (4 in) narrower than the width.

1 Sew any fabric and lining widths if required with plain seams pressed open. Place the lining to the fabric with right sides facing and the top of the lining 4 cm (1$\frac{1}{2}$ in) below the top of the curtain fabric. Arrange the side edges evenly and stitch the lining to the fabric 1.5 cm ($\frac{5}{8}$ in) in from the raw edges, finishing the stitching above the hem level (diagram 1).

DIAGRAM 1

2 Turn the curtain right side out. The narrower lining will pull the side edges of the curtain over to the wrong side for 2.5 cm (1 in). Arrange the hems evenly on both side edges and press in place (diagram 2).

DIAGRAM 2

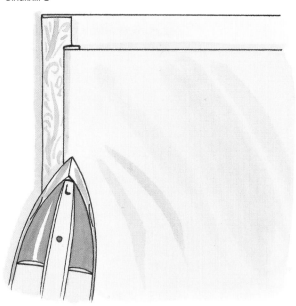

3 Press 4 cm (1½ in) over to the wrong side at the top edge of the curtain. Cut a length of heading tape 5 cm (2 in) longer than the curtain width and, with wrong sides facing, place it 3 mm (⅛ in) below the top edge of the curtain. Turn under the ends of the heading tape 2.5 cm (1 in) at each side edge, level with the edge of the curtain (diagram 3).

DIAGRAM 3

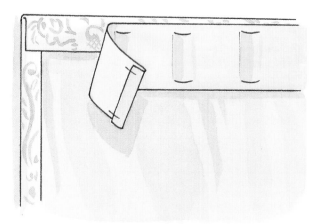

4 Stitch the heading tape in place up the side edge, across one long edge of the tape and down the opposite side edge. Stitch the other edge of the tape in the same way, so that the ends are stitched twice to ensure the cords are caught firmly in the stitching (diagram 4).

DIAGRAM 4

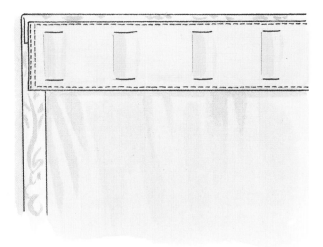

5 Trim the lower edge of the lining 2 cm (¾ in) shorter than the lower edge of the curtains. Press a 7.5 cm (3 in) double hem to the wrong side on the curtain and stitch in place (diagram 5).

DIAGRAM 5

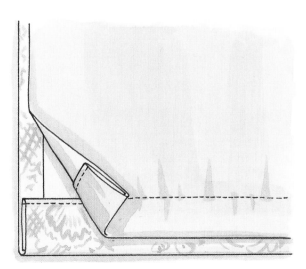

6 Make the lining hem in the same way so that it faces the curtain hem. Finish stitching the lining to the side hems by hand (diagram 6). Gather the curtains along the top edge, see Cord tidies and curtain weights, page 120.

DIAGRAM 6

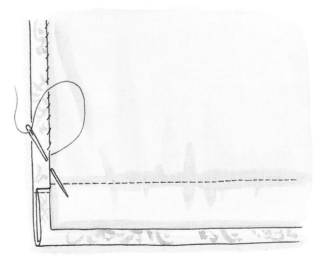

Loose-lined curtains

Loose-lined curtains are hemmed along the side edges of the fabric before the lining is attached. The lining is then stitched to the hems by hand, but left loose across the width of the curtain. You can stitch the hems at the sides and across the lower edge of the curtain by hand or machine. Stitching by hand gives a finer finish, whereas machine stitching is quicker and more durable. For large curtains, it is well worthwhile mastering the machined blind hemstitch, see page 15.

MATERIALS
Curtain fabric
Sewing thread
Lining fabric
Heading tape

CUTTING OUT

1.5 cm (⅝ in) seam allowances are included unless instructions state otherwise.

Calculate the fabric amount as for the Tube-lined curtains, page 114. For the width, allow 6 cm (2¼ in) for each side hem and 3 cm (1¼ in) for each seam, if you are using more than one width of fabric. For the length, add on 4 cm (1½ in) for the top hem and 15–40 cm (6–16 in) for the lower hem. Cut the lining 4 cm (1½ in) shorter than the curtain fabric at the top edge and 12 cm (4¾ in) narrower than the width.

1 Join fabric and lining widths if required with plain seams pressed open. Press a 3 cm (1¼ in) wide double hem to the wrong side along the side edges of the curtain. Stitch in place by hand or machine.

2 Press 2 cm (¾ in) to the wrong side along the side edges of the lining. Place the lining to the wrong side of the curtains so that the lining edges overlap the side hems by 1 cm (⅜ in) and the top of the lining is 4 cm (1½ in) down from the top of the curtain.

3 Handstitch the lining to the side hems, finishing the stitching above the top of the lower hem. Trim the lining 3 cm (1¼ in) shorter than the fabric at the lower edge (diagram 1).

DIAGRAM 1

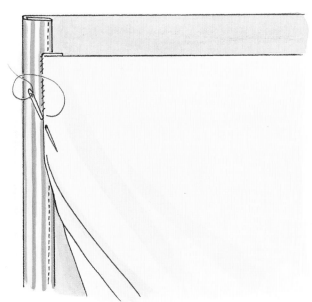

4 Press 4 cm (1½ in) to the wrong side across the top edge and stitch on the heading tape in the same way as for the Tube-lined curtains, steps 3 and 4, page 116.

5 Press a double hem of the required depth to the wrong side. Unfold the hem and the unstitched part of the side hem. At one side edge, press the corner in at an angle on a line that begins at the side edge on the top fold and intersects the inner edge of the side hem at the lower fold (diagram 2).

DIAGRAM 2

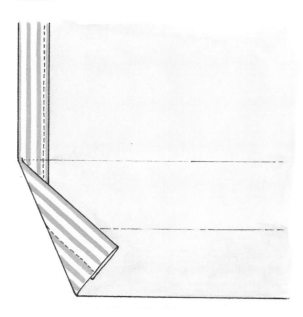

6 Refold the hem so that it forms a neat miter at the corner. Miter the other corner in the same way. Handstitch the miters in place and stitch the hem in place by hand or machine (diagram 3).

DIAGRAM 3

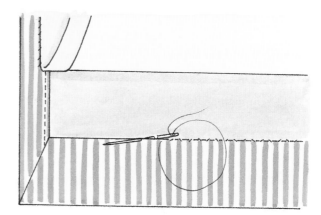

CORD TIDIES AND CURTAIN WEIGHTS

To gather curtains, pull all cords simultaneously at the center of the heading tape and gradually push the gathers or pleats away to each side. Once the curtain is fully gathered or pleated, the cords can be wrapped neatly around a cord tidy.

Curtain weights add weight to the hems of large curtains to improve their hang. They come in two forms: round, coin-like weights and long, string-like weights. The coins are retained in small fabric pouches, which are stitched inside the hem at each corner and at the base of any seams, if you are using more than one width of fabric. The string-like weights sit in the base of the hem and are attached with light stitching at the corners and seams.

7 Make a double hem on the lining the same depth as the one on the curtain and machine stitch it in place. Finish stitching the side edges of the lining to the curtain side hems by hand (diagram 4). Gather the curtains along the top edge, see below.

DIAGRAM **4**

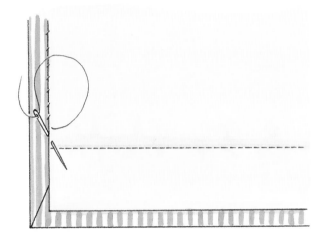

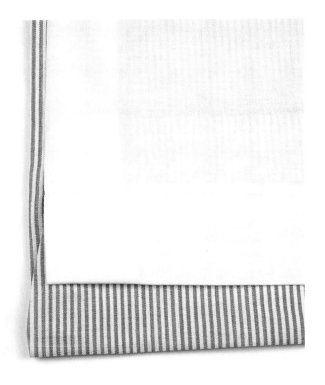

Interlined curtain

Interlining is a layer of specially made soft fabric that is sandwiched between the curtain fabric and the lining. It adds weight to lightweight fabric and gives a sumptuous finish to the curtains. Interlined curtains also help reduce draughts and keep out the cold.

MATERIALS
Curtain fabric
Sewing thread
Interlining
Lining fabric
Heading tape

CUTTING OUT

1.5 cm ($^5/_8$ in) seam allowances are included unless instructions state otherwise.

Calculate the fabric amount as for the Tube-lined curtains, page 114. For the width, allow 6 cm (2$^1/_2$ in) for each side hem and 3 cm (1$^1/_4$ in) for each join. For the length, add on 4 cm (1$^1/_2$ in) for the top hem and 12 cm (4$^3/_4$ in) for the lower hem. Cut the lining fabric and interlining to the same size.

NOTE

The interlining is held in place against the curtain fabric with lines of lockstitch, see page 13, worked from the top to the base of the curtain. Curtains made from one fabric width should be lockstitched a third of the width in from each side. Wider curtains, made from more than one fabric width, should be lockstitched at each seam and twice between each seam, as well as between the outer seams and the side edges of the curtain. A thick interlining may need to be trimmed along the fold of the lower hem to reduce bulk.

1 Join fabric and lining widths if required with plain seams pressed open. If required, join interlining widths by butting the edges together and stitching across the join with herringbone stitch, see page 13.

2 Place the curtain fabric right side down on a worktop and smooth it out flat. Place the interlining on top with edges and seams lined up.

3 Fold back the interlining to the furthest seam or position of lockstitch line. Lockstitch the interlining to the fabric from 5 cm (2 in) below the top edge to the lower edge, picking up just a thread of curtain fabric so that the stitching does not show. Space the stitches wide apart and do not pull them tight (diagram 1).

DIAGRAM 1

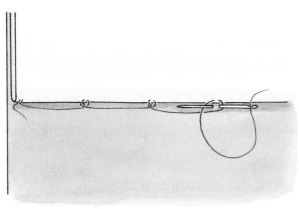

4 When the first line of lockstitch is complete, smooth the interlining back across the fabric to the position for the next lockstitch line and lockstitch in the same way. Repeat until all lines of lockstitch are complete.

5 Fold both interlining and fabric together over to the wrong side for 6 cm (2½ in) along both side edges. At the lower edge, fold a 12 cm (4¾ in) hem to the wrong side. Mark the inner edge of each hem at the corner where they intersect (diagram 2).

DIAGRAM 2

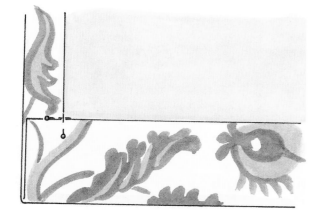

6 Open out the hems and refold the corner diagonally to the wrong side between the marked points. If you are using heavy interlining, trim it along the pressed line (diagram 3).

DIAGRAM 3

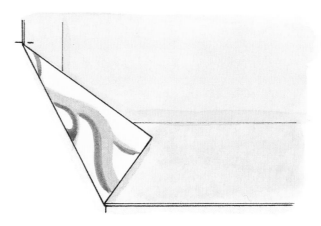

7 Refold the hems to form a mitered corner. Stitch along the side edges with long stitch, see page 13, spacing the stitches about 4 cm (1½ in) apart and taking the stitches through both layers of interlining but not the main fabric.

8 Slipstitch the edges of the corner miteres together. Stitch the lower hem with 2 cm (¾ in) long herring-bone stitches (diagram 4).

DIAGRAM 4

9 Place the lining centrally on top of the interlining with raw edges matching along the top edge. Lockstitch it in place in the same way as the interlining, finishing the stitching above the hem and 5 cm (2 in) down from the top edge. Trim the side edges of the lining level with the edges of the curtain. Tuck under the raw edges along the sides of the lining so that 3 cm (1¼ in) of curtain side hem shows. Pin and slip hem the lining in place along the side edges to just above the lower hem, see page 12.

DIAGRAM 5

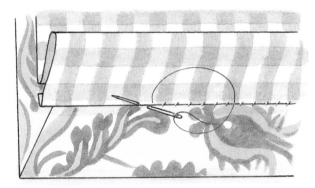

10 Trim the lining to 6 cm (2½ in) longer than the curtain. Press 1.5 cm (⅝ in) to the wrong side along the lower edge of the lining. Pin in place so the raw edge of the lining is level with the raw edge of the hem and slip hem the lining to the hem along the pressed edge (diagram 5).

DIAGRAM 6

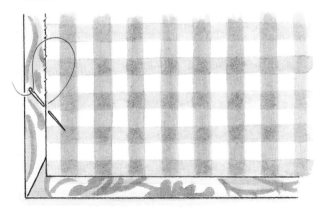

11 Allow the excess lining to fall downwards, forming a pleat. Finish stitching the lining to the side hems down to the bottom of the lining (diagram 6).

12 At the top edge of the curtain, fold back the lining and trim the interlining 4 cm (1½ in) below the top edge (diagram 7). Fold both the lining and fabric over to the wrong side for 4 cm (1½ in) along the top edge. Stitch on the heading tape in the same way as for the Tube-lined curtains, steps 3 and 4, page 116. Gather the curtains along the top edge, see Cord tidies and curtain weights, page 120.

DIAGRAM 7

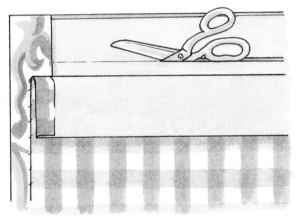

Shaped tieback

This formal style of tieback has an elegant curved shape and is made by covering stiff interfacing, valance interfacing or buckram with fabric that matches or contrasts with the curtain. The tiebacks can be left untrimmed or finished with cord or piping around the outer edge. They are fixed to a hook on the wall by two small rings.

TIEBACKS

First work out the required length and width of the curved tieback – the pattern illustrated is for a tieback about 28 cm (11 in) long and 12 cm (5 in) wide at the fold. Draw the pattern for half the shape of the tieback on a large piece of folded paper. Cut out the shape through both layers of paper, then open out the pattern to its full length. Try the pattern on the curtain to check the length and fit, and adjust the size and smoothness of the curve as required.

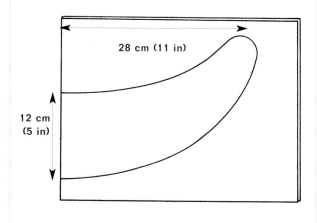

28 cm (11 in)

12 cm (5 in)

CUTTING OUT

1.5 cm ($^5/_8$ in) seam allowances are included unless instructions state otherwise.

Cut out the front fabric 1.5 cm ($^5/_8$ in) larger than the pattern all round. Cut out the lining fabric and interlining 6 mm ($^1/_4$ in) larger than the pattern all round. Cut the heavyweight iron-on interfacing or buckram to the pattern size.

MATERIALS
Curtain fabric
Sewing thread
Heavyweight iron-on interfacing or buckram
Interlining
Lining fabric
Cord (optional)
4 small rings (two for each tieback)
2 wall hooks

1 Center the heavyweight iron-on interfacing, fusible side up, on the interlining and pin in place. Snip the projecting fabric at curves and snip out notches around the ends.

2 Fold the projecting edges of the interlining over onto the iron-on interfacing and press to fuse them in place. Take care to press on the interlining only and remove pins as you reach them (diagram 1).

DIAGRAM 1

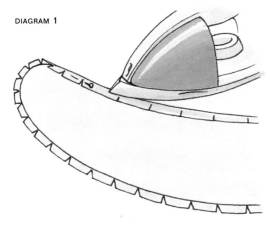

3 Pin the interlined piece, fusible side up, on the wrong side of the fabric. Snip and notch the fabric edges and fuse them in place in the same way as the interlining (diagram 2).

DIAGRAM 2

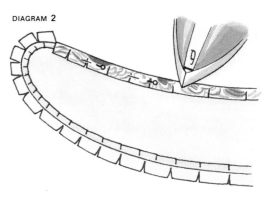

4 Snip and notch 6 mm ($^1/_4$ in) into the edge of the lining. Press 6 mm ($^1/_4$ in) to the wrong side all round the lining. Pin the lining to the wrong side of the tieback and handstitch in place around the edges (diagram 3).

DIAGRAM 3

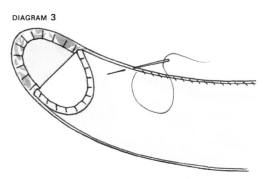

5 If you require a cord trim, handstitch the cord around the edge of the tieback, finishing the ends inside the lining in an inconspicuous place. Stitch small rings to the wrong side of the tieback at each end to fasten onto a hook on the wall.

Straight tieback

This simple straight tieback looks very effective on curtains that are partially drawn back and pulled up into a swag. It can be fastened with eyelets or rings to a hook beside the window.

MATERIALS
Curtain fabric
Sewing thread
Heavyweight iron-on interfacing
Large eyelets

CUTTING OUT
1.5 cm ($^5/_8$ in) seam allowances are included unless instructions state otherwise.

Cut the tieback 10 cm (4 in) wide by the required length plus 3 cm ($^5/_8$ in) all round. Cut the interfacing to same length but half the width.

1 Apply the iron-on interfacing lengthways to the wrong side of half the fabric. Fold the tieback in half lengthways with right sides facing. Stitch across each short edge and along the long edge, leaving a 10 cm (4 in) opening partway along the long edge (diagram 1).

DIAGRAM 1

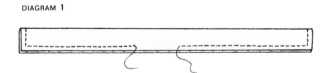

2 Trim the seams and corners and turn the tieback right side out. Press the seam at the edge and press the seam allowance inside along the opening. Slipstitch the opening closed.

3 Following the manufacturer's instructions, attach an eyelet centrally at each end of the tieback to fasten onto a hook on the wall (diagram 2).

DIAGRAM 2

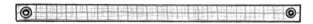

Eyelet café curtain

This simple café curtain is made from a basic rectangle of fabric trimmed with a fabric flap along the top edge. It is threaded onto a narrow pole through large metal eyelets.

MATERIALS
Lightweight curtain fabric
Sewing thread
Large eyelets

CUTTING OUT

1.5 cm ($^5/_8$ in) seam allowances are included unless instructions state otherwise.

Measure the required finished size, then add on 20 cm (8 in) to the width for fullness and hems, and 9.5 cm ($3^3/_4$ in) to the length. Cut out the main piece to this size. Cut the flap the same width by a third of the curtain length plus 3.5 cm ($1^3/_8$ in).

1 Press 1 cm ($^3/_8$ in) double hems to the wrong side along both side edges of the main piece and stitch in place. Press a double 4 cm ($1^1/_2$ in) hem across the lower edge and stitch in place.

NOTE
When attaching the eyelets, work on a solid surface – concrete or similar.

2 Press 1 cm ($^3/_8$ in) double hems to the wrong side along the sides and lower edge of the flap and stitch in place. Place the right side of the flap to the wrong side of curtain with the top edges level and stitch together across the top edge (diagram 1). Turn the flap over to the right side and press.

DIAGRAM **1**

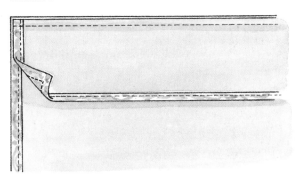

3 Mark the eyelet positions 2 cm ($^3/_4$ in) down from the top and 2 cm ($^3/_4$ in) in from the side edges. Space the others evenly about 13 cm (5 in) apart. Attach the eyelets through the double fabric layer, following the manufacturer's instructions (diagram 2).

DIAGRAM **2**

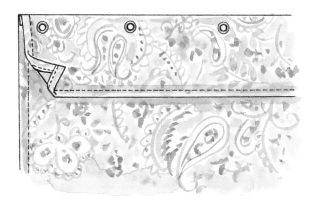

Self-frill café curtain

This curtain has a casing along the top so that it can be gathered onto a pole or wire. The narrow fold of fabric above the casing forms a pretty self frill.

MATERIALS
Lightweight curtain fabric
Sewing thread
Curtain pole or tension rod

CUTTING OUT

1.5 cm (⁵⁄₈ in) seam allowances are included unless instructions state otherwise.

Measure the width across the pole and the required length from the pole to the sill. Cut the curtain twice the pole width by the required length plus 18 cm (7 in).

1 Press a 1 cm (³⁄₈ in) double hem to the wrong side along both side edges of the curtain and stitch in place.

2 Press 1 cm (³⁄₈ in), then 6 cm (2¹⁄₄ in) to the wrong side across the top edge. Stitch along the pressed edge and again 3 cm (1¹⁄₄ in) above it to form a casing (diagram 1).

DIAGRAM **1**

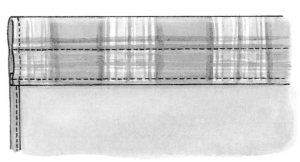

3 At the lower edge, press a double 4 cm (1¹⁄₂ in) hem to the wrong side and stitch in place.

Café curtain with ties

Fabric ties are used to attach this stylish curtain to a pole. The fabric is finished with a scalloped edge or an alternative hem could be made.

MATERIALS
Lightweight curtain fabric with optional scalloped edge
Sewing thread
Tension rod or curtain pole

CUTTING OUT

1.5 cm ($^5/_8$ in) seam allowances are included unless instructions state otherwise.

Measure the required finished size, then add 14 cm ($5^1/_2$ in) to the width for fullness and hems. Add 9.5 cm ($3^3/_4$ in) to the length, or just 1.5 cm ($^5/_8$ in) if the lower edge is ready finished. Cut out the main piece to this size. Cut a facing 2 cm ($^3/_4$ in) wider than the finished size by 6.5 cm ($2^5/_8$ in) deep. Cut ties 50 cm ($19^3/_4$ in) by 4 cm ($1^1/_2$ in).

1 Press 1 cm ($^3/_8$ in) wide double hems to the wrong side along both side edges of the main piece and stitch in place.

2 Press 1 cm ($^3/_8$ in) to the wrong side around all edges of the ties. Press the ties in half lengthways and stitch along the long edges.

3 Fold the ties in half. With the fold 6 mm ($^1/_4$ in) down from the top edge and the ends pointing downwards, pin the ties to the right side of the main piece about 15 cm (6 in) apart. Tack the ties in place.

4 Place the facing across the top edge of the main piece with right sides together and raw edges level, allowing it to project 1 cm ($^3/_8$ in) at each end. Stitch in place across the top edge and trim the seam to 1 cm ($^3/_8$ in) (diagram 1) .

DIAGRAM 1

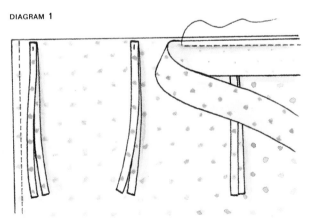

5 Press 1 cm ($^3/_8$ in) to the wrong side around the other edges of the facing. Fold the facing over to the wrong side and press the seam at the edge. Stitch around the side and lower edges of the facing. If required, press a 4 cm ($1^1/_2$ in) double hem to the wrong side across the lower edge of the curtain and stitch in place.

Voile swag

A simple length of fine linen, voile, or muslin will drape beautifully over a pole to make an amazingly simple but effective window treatment. A single drape looped behind the pole at each end will frame a window perfectly. Alternatively, you can experiment with more elaborate options. First fix the pole, then drape the fabric over to establish the length required.

MATERIALS
Fine curtain fabric
Sewing thread
Double-sided adhesive foam pads (optional)

1 Stitch across the fabric ends with a close zigzag stitch.

2 Arrange the drape over the pole. If it slips out of place, use adhesive foam pads to secure the fabric to the pole at the back where they will not be visible.

Swag variations

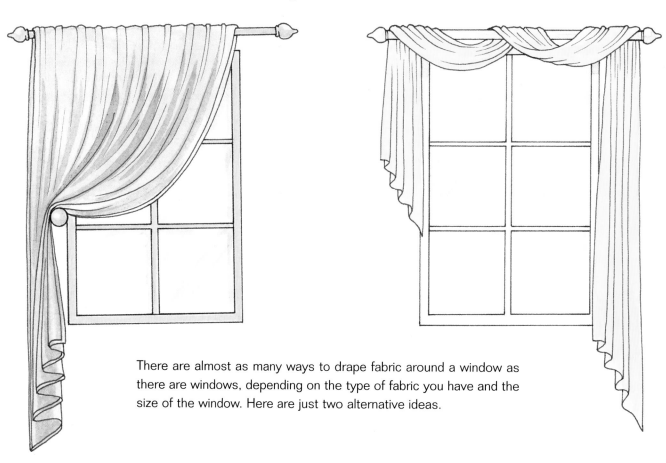

There are almost as many ways to drape fabric around a window as there are windows, depending on the type of fabric you have and the size of the window. Here are just two alternative ideas.

Valance with fold-over casing

This neat valance provides a pretty country-style treatment for a small window in a recess. It is also useful to soften the effect of a bare kitchen window, where curtains might intrude onto the work surface. The top edge is finished with a simple fold-over casing through which a tension rod is inserted to support the pelmet within the recess.

MATERIALS
Curtain fabric
Sewing thread
Lining fabric
Tension rod

CUTTING OUT

1.5 cm ($^5/_8$ in) seam allowances are included unless instructions state otherwise.

Measure the length of the rod and cut the fabric width to twice this measurement plus 3 cm ($1^1/_4$ in) for side seams. Decide on the depth of the valance and add 7 cm ($2^3/_4$ in) for hems. Cut the lining to the same width as the main fabric, but 8 cm ($3^1/_4$ in) shorter.

1   Place the lining fabric and main fabric together with right sides facing and lower edges level. Stitch together across the lower edge (diagram 1).

DIAGRAM 1

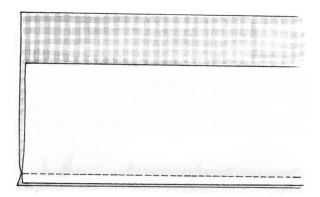

2   Open out and press the seam allowances towards the lining. Refold with right sides facing so that the seam is 5 mm ($^1/_4$ in) above the fold on the lining side. Stitch together along the side edges (diagram 2).

DIAGRAM 2

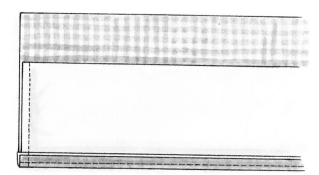

3 Turn right side out. Press 1 cm (^{3}⁄$_8$ in) to the wrong side along the top edge of the fabric. Then press 4 cm (1^1⁄$_2$ in) to the wrong side along the top edge, so that it overlaps the top edge of the lining to form a casing.

4 Stitch the casing in place along its lower edge and again just inside the top fold edge (diagram 3).

DIAGRAM 3

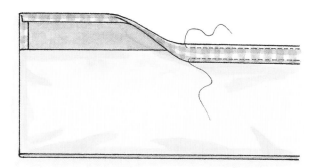

Pencil pleat valance

This more formal style of valance is finished with heading tape at the top and is drawn up into pleats or gathers. A special type of curtain track is available with an extra rail from which you can hang the valance. Alternatively, you can fix the valance with Velcro to a narrow valance shelf with rounded front corners. This is secured to the wall above the window.

MATERIALS
Curtain fabric
Sewing thread
Lining fabric
Heading tape
Curtain hooks or Half-and-half Velcro tape

1 Place the lining and fabric together with right sides facing and lower edges level. Stitch together across the lower edge.

2 Open out and press the seam allowances towards the lining. Refold with right sides facing so that the seam is 1 cm (^{3}⁄$_8$ in) above the fold on the lining side. Stitch together along the side edges (diagram 1).

DIAGRAM 1

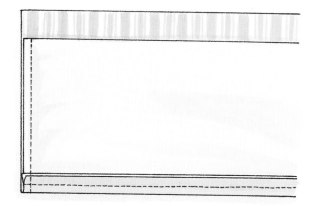

CUTTING OUT

1.5 cm (^{5}⁄$_8$ in) seam allowances are included unless instructions state otherwise.

Calculate the number of fabric widths required for the valance in the same way as for Tube-lined curtains, page 114. Decide on the depth of the valance and add 6.5 cm (2^1⁄$_2$ in) for hems. Cut the lining pieces to the same width as the main fabric, but 6 cm (2^1⁄$_4$ in) shorter.

3 Turn right side out. Press 4 cm (1 ½ in) over to the wrong side along the top edge. Stitch on the heading tape in the same way as for Tube-lined curtains, steps 3 and 4, page 116 (diagram 2). Pull up the heading tape to the required width and arrange the fullness evenly.

4 If you are hanging the valance from a track, insert curtain hooks. If you are using a pelmet shelf, cut the Velcro to fit around the edge of the shelf. Stick the adhesive side of the Velcro to the edge of the shelf. Place the "stitch" part to the wrong side of the heading tape and handstitch in place to the back folds of the pleats or gathers.

DIAGRAM 2

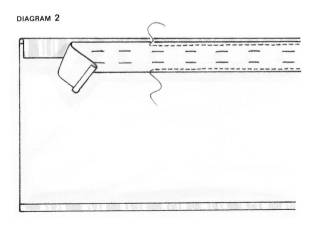

Door curtain

A lightweight door curtain is a useful accessory for a door with a glass panel, as it provides privacy while still letting the light in. A door curtain also gives a stylish look to a cupboard with a glass panel door. The curtain is held taut at top and bottom by lengths of plastic-covered tension wire secured with metal screw eyes hooked onto small screw hooks on the door.

MATERIALS
Lightweight fabric
Sewing thread
Tension wire
Screw hooks and eyes

CUTTING OUT

1.5 cm ($^5/_8$ in) seam allowances are included unless instructions state otherwise.
Measure the required width and double it for fullness.
Measure the length and add on 6 cm ($2^1/_4$ in) for hems. Cut out the fabric to these measurements.

1 Press 1 cm ($^3/_8$ in) wide double hems along both side edges. Stitch in place (diagram 1).

DIAGRAM 1

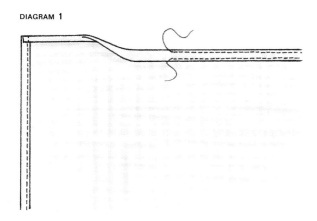

2 At the top and lower edges, press 1 cm ($^3/_8$ in), then 2 cm ($^3/_4$ in) to the wrong side to make casings. Stitch in place along both edges of the casing (diagram 2). Insert lengths of tension wire into the casings.

DIAGRAM 2

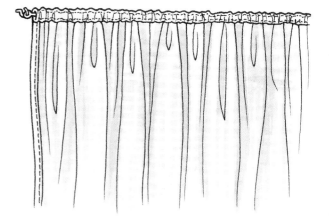

Basic roller blind

A roller blind is one of the simplest window treatments. It consists of a piece of stiffened fabric that hangs from a roller at the top and wraps neatly around it when the blind is raised. A roller blind can be hung alone or used as a sunshade in conjunction with curtains. Roller blinds are ideal for the kitchen and bathroom, where curtains might drag on a work surface or become splashed.

MATERIALS
Medium-weight fabric
Stiffening solution or spray
Roller blind kit

CUTTING OUT

Cut the fabric to about 2 in (5 cm) wider than required by 12 in (30 cm) longer to allow for the lower hem and to wrap around the roller. Ensure that the edges are straight and check that the side edges are at right angles to the top edge by using a protractor. If you do not have this tool, refer to diagram 1 – if A to B measures three units, A to C equals four units and B to C equals five units, the angle will be a right angle. Any fabric pulled or printed off grain will not roll evenly and should be avoided.

NOTE

There are two main types of roller blind: those operated by a tension roller and those with a side winder mechanism. The latter are the more widely available and usually come as a kit containing the roller, fixing brackets, winding mechanism and batten for the lower edge.

Before you make up the blind, spray or soak the fabric to stiffen it and prevent the side edges from fraying. There are various products on the market for these purposes. The soaking method is generally thought to be the more successful of the two. The fabric should not come right to the end of the roller. Leave a gap of 2 cm (³⁄₄ in) between the fabric and the side walls on a blind to be hung in a recess.

DIAGRAM 1

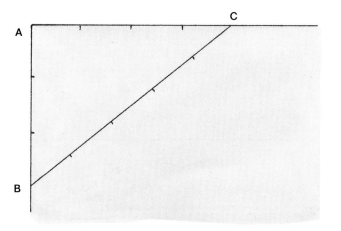

1 Stiffen the fabric with a stiffening solution or spray, following the manufacturer's instructions. When the fabric is stiffened, trim the side edges so that the blind is the required width. Press 1 cm (³⁄₈ in), then 3.5 cm (1³⁄₈ in) to the wrong side across the lower edge and stitch in place to make a channel for the batten.

2 Secure the fabric to the roller (which is usually supplied with a length of double-sided adhesive tape stuck to it for this purpose). Insert the batten into the channel and screw on the blind pull. Fix the blind in position inside or outside the window recess, as required.

Roller blind variations

ROLLER BLIND WITH EYELET TRIM

Prepare the fabric and make up the blind as for the Basic roller blind, page 142. Determine the positions for the eyelets, placing them about 12 cm (4¾ in) up from the lower edge and spaced about 15 cm (6 in) apart. Insert the eyelets, following the manufacturer's instructions.

ROLLER BLIND WITH SCALLOPED BORDER

Stiffen the fabric and trim to the required width. Draw out the shape of the scallops on a paper pattern, adjusting their size to fit across the desired width. The scallops shown are 7 cm (2¾ in) deep and 38 cm (15 in) wide. Cut a 5 cm (2 in) wide bias strip and bind the scalloped edge, see Bias binding, page 16. With right sides facing, fold the blind 7 cm (2¾ in) above the top of the binding and stitch 3.5 cm (1⅜ in) in from the fold. Press the stitched pleat down to make a channel for the batten. Make up the blind as for the Basic roller blind, step 2, page 142.

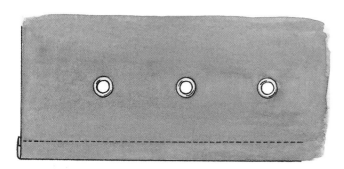

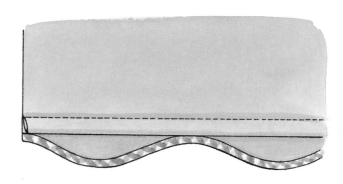

ROLLER BLIND WITH SHAPED EDGE AND DOWEL ROD

Stiffen the fabric and trim to the required width. Press 18 cm (7 in) to the wrong side across the lower edge. If the fabric is still tending to fray, apply iron-on buckram to the pressed-back turning. Stitch 5 mm (¼ in) down from the cut edge of the pressed-back turning, then again 3.5 cm (1⅜ in) below that to make a channel for the batten. Draw a paper pattern, adjusting the size and number of cutouts to fit across the width of the blind. The cutouts shown are 18 cm (7 in) wide, 6.5 cm (2½ in) deep and 5 cm (2 in) apart. Mark and cut out the cutouts. Stitch across 2 cm (¾ in) up from the folds to make channels to thread a dowel rod through. Make up the blind as for the Basic roller blind, step 2, page 142.

ROLLER BLIND WITH LACE TRIM

Stiffen the fabric and trim to the required width. Press 1 cm (⅜ in), then 4 cm (1½ in) to the wrong side across the lower edge and stitch in place. Lap the top edge of the lace under the lower edge of the hem and stitch in place. Make up the blind as for the Basic roller blind, step 2, page 142.

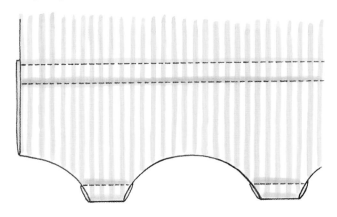

Roman blind

A Roman blind lies flat when it is lowered, but concertinas into elegant pleats across its width when raised. The pleats are created by thin lengths of dowel inserted into casings at the back of the blind and pulled up by a system of rings and cords.

MATERIALS
Closely woven upholstery fabric
Sewing thread
Wooden batten, 30 mm (1¼ in) square
Screw eyes
Half-and-half Velcro tape
Blind rings
Lengths of dowel, 6 mm (¼ in) in diameter
Lath, 30 x 6 mm (1¼ x ¼ in)
Cleat (to hold cords in place)
Blind cord and acorn

PREPARATION
The blind is attached with Velcro to a wooden batten fixed to the wall above the window. Prepare the batten as follows. Fix a screw eye 10 cm (4 in), or 15 cm (6 in) for a wider blind, from each end of the wooden batten, placing it midway between the front and back edges. This will be the underside. Fix another screw eye, again placing it centrally, 1.5 cm (⅝ in) from the end where the cord will be used to pull the blind up. If the window is wide, add another supporting screw eye at the center of the batten. Stick the adhesive half of the Velcro across the front of the batten. Fix the batten above the window, using a spirit level to ensure it is straight. Fix the cleat to the wall.

1 Press 1 cm (⅜ in), then 4 cm (1½ in) deep hems to the wrong side along both side edges. Stitch the hems in place close to the inner fold (diagram 1).

2 Press a 1 cm (⅜ in), then 5 cm (2 in) hem to the wrong side across the lower edge. Stitch the hem in place close to the inner fold. Leave the side edges of the hem open (diagram 1).

CUTTING OUT
1.5 cm (⅝ in) seam allowances are included unless instructions state otherwise.

Before cutting out, decide how many casing rods you will need. Allow about 25–33 cm (10–13 in) between the rods and half this distance between the top of the lower hem and the first casing.

For the width of the blind, measure across the front of the batten and add on 10 cm (4 in). For the length, measure from the top of the batten to the window sill, add on 3 cm (1¼ in) for each dowel casing and 7 cm (2¾ in) for turnings.

3 Mark the casing positions on the wrong side of the fabric with two parallel lines spaced 3 cm (1¼ in) apart (diagram 1).

DIAGRAM 1

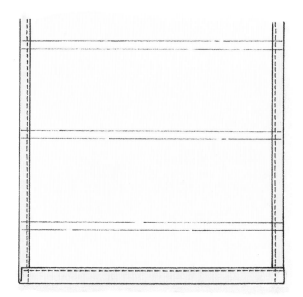

4 With right sides together, fold the fabric along the center between the lines so that the lines match. Stitch along the lines to form 1.5 cm (⅝ in) deep casings. Stitch all the casings in this way.

5 Using a double thread, stitch a ring to the fold of each casing 10 cm (4 in) in from each side edge on a narrow blind, and 15 cm (6 in) in from each side edge on a wider blind (diagram 2).

DIAGRAM 2

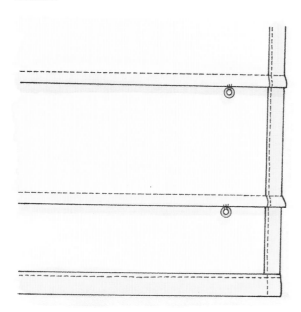

6 Press 1 cm (⅜ in) to the wrong side across the top edge of the blind. Pin the "stitch" half of the Velcro across the top edge to cover the turning and stitch in place around all four edges (diagram 3).

DIAGRAM 3

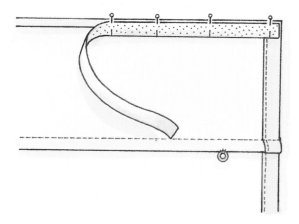

7 Insert a length of dowel into each casing and hand-stitch the ends of the casings closed. Insert the lath into the hem at the lower edge of the blind and hand-stitch the ends closed.

8 Tie a cord to the lowest ring on the opposite side to the cleat and thread up through the rings to the top. Then allow enough cord to go across the top of the blind and down the cleat side to reach the cleat (diagram 4).

9 In the same way, thread a separate cord up through the rings near the opposite edge, allowing enough cord to go across and down to the cleat. This will be shorter than the first cord (diagram 4).

10 Attach the Velcro on the blind to the Velcro on the wall batten. Thread the cords through the screw eyes as shown (diagram 4). Pull the cords to raise the blind and fasten around the cleat. Trim the cords if required, thread on the acorn and knot the ends below it.

DIAGRAM 4

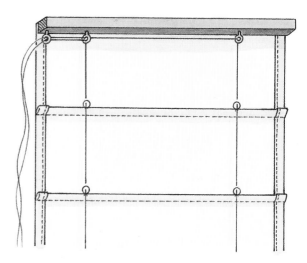

NOTE

As well as plain fabrics, vertical stripes or small prints work well for a Roman blind. Avoid horizontal stripes and any large prints, as the horizontal casings will cut across the design.

Roman blind variations

BLIND WITH MITERED BORDER

A neat mitered border gives a crisp edge to a Roman blind for a smart, contemporary look. The border is most effective if it is visible when the blind is pulled up. To achieve this, allow the same distance between the finished lower edge and the first casing as between the other casings.

When cutting out, allow a seam allowance only at the side edges of the blind. Stitch the outer edge of the border to the wrong side of the blind down the side edges. Stitch the lower border to the right side across the lower edge so the stitching is level with the top of the hem allowance. Snip into the side seam allowance at the top of the hem and join the border corners, see Mitered borders, page 22. Make the hem, keeping the border out of the way, then topstitch the inner edge of the border in place. The casings are then stitched across the border.

BLIND WITH PINTUCKED LOWER EDGE

A panel of tucks adds discreet but stylish detail to a plain blind. Use bold, contrasting topstitching on the right side of the tucks to highlight the detail. To ensure the tucks are visible when the blind is pulled up, allow the same distance between the finished lower edge and the first casing as between the other casings.

When working out the length of the blind, add twice the finished depth of the tucks multiplied by the number of tucks.

Make the hems at the sides and lower edge of the blind, then stitch the tucks so that the fold of each tuck is just above the stitching of the previous tuck, see Tucks, page 27.

Quick Roman blind

This quick version of the Roman blind pulls up into concertina pleats in a similar way to the traditional Roman blind, but does not use the same system of dowels and rings. Instead, just one length of dowel is used in the lowest casing and fine cords are stitched through the casings on the wrong side to pull the blind up. If you wish to make the blind firmer, you could insert stiff wires into the casings. Work out the positions and spacing of the casings in the same way as for the Roman blind, page 146.

MATERIALS
Closely woven upholstery fabric
Sewing thread
Wooden batten, 30 mm (1¼ in) square
Screw eyes
Half-and-half Velcro tape
Dowel, 6 mm (¼ in) in diameter
Cleat (to hold cords in place)
Fine cord and acorn

CUTTING OUT

1.5 cm (⅝ in) seam allowances are included unless instructions state otherwise.

Measure the required width and add on 6 cm (2¼ in). For the length, measure from the top of the batten to the window sill and add on 2 cm (¾ in) for each casing plus 4 cm (1½ in) for turnings.

2 Measure and mark parallel lines across the blind the required distance apart for the casings (diagram 1).

3 With right sides together, fold the blind along the marked lines and stitch across 1 cm (⅜ in) away from each fold. Slip the dowel into the lowest casing and handstitch across each end of the casing (diagram 2).

DIAGRAM 2

1 Press 1 cm (⅜ in), then 2 cm (¾ in) hems to the wrong side along both side edges. Stitch the hems in place close to the inner fold. Make a hem across the lower edge in the same way (diagram 1).

DIAGRAM 1

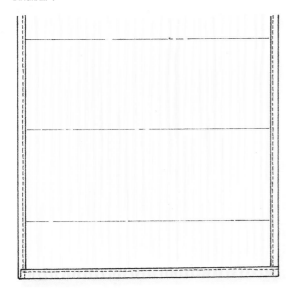

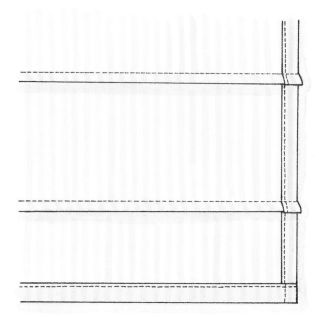

4 Press 1 cm ($^3/_8$ in) over to the wrong side across the top edge. Place the "stitch" half of the Velcro across to cover the raw edge. Pin and stitch the Velcro in place around all four edges (diagram 3).

DIAGRAM **3**

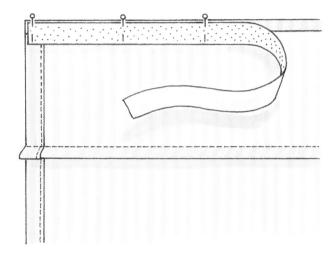

5 Allow enough cord to go up the blind, across the top of the blind, and down the cleat side to reach the cleat. Make a large knot at the end of the cord and thread the cord into a needle. Stitch the cord through the center of the lower casing, 10 cm (4 in) in from the side edge (diagram 4).

6 Then stitch through each of the casings above it in the same way. Stitch a separate cord through the casings on the opposite edge in the same way (diagram 4).

DIAGRAM **4**

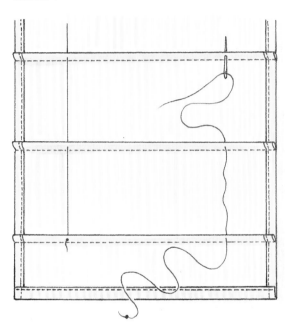

7 Hang the blind in the same way as the Roman blind, step 10, page 148.

London blind

This type of blind has a soft, ruched appearance and looks best on windows where the blind is left lowered for most of the time so that the gently gathered fabric is displayed to advantage. To retain the ruched effect even when the blind is pulled down, allow extra length when cutting out the fabric. Choose a fairly densely woven upholstery fabric for a London blind – plain and small prints work well.

MATERIALS
Closely woven upholstery fabric
Sewing thread
Wooden batten, 30 mm (1 1/4 in) square
Screw eyes
Half-and-half Velcro tape
Dowel or lath, 1 cm (3/8 in) in diameter
Blind cord, blind rings, and acorn
Cleat (to hold cords in place)
2 tassels (optional)

PREPARATION
Prepare the batten for hanging in the same way as for the Roman blind, page 146, but aligning the screw eyes with the rings.

CUTTING OUT
1.5 cm (5/8 in) seam allowances are included unless instructions state otherwise.

For the width of the blind, measure across the front of the batten and add on 40 cm (16 in) for the pleats and side hems. For the length, measure from the top of the batten to the window sill and add on 6 cm (2 1/4 in).

1 Press 1 cm (3/8 in), then 4 cm (1 1/2 in) hems to the wrong side around the side and lower edges of the blind. Miter the corners as in Mitered hem, page 23. Stitch the hems in place (diagram 1).

2 On the wrong side of the top edge, measure and mark 20 cm (8 in) and 35 cm (13 3/4 in) in from one side edge. Measure and mark the same distances in from the other side edge (diagram 1).

DIAGRAM 1

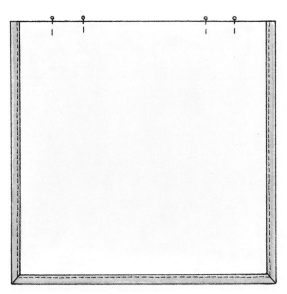

3   Fold the fabric vertically with right sides facing to match the first two marks. Stitch for 5 cm (2 in) down from the top edge to form an inverted pleat. Stitch a second inverted pleat at the other side of the fabric in the same way (diagram 2).

4   Open out each pleat and arrange centrally behind the stitching, then press in place just at the top, see Pleats, page 26 (diagram 2).

DIAGRAM **2**

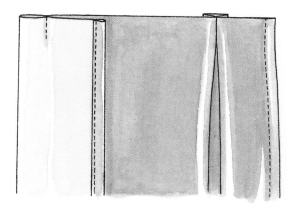

5   Press 1 cm ($^3/_8$ in) to the wrong side across the top edge of the blind. Pin the "stitch" part of the Velcro across the top edge to cover the turning and stitch in place around all four edges (diagram 3).

DIAGRAM **3**

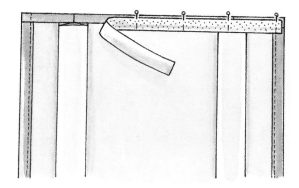

6   On the wrong side, lightly mark a line 20 cm (8 in) in from each side edge in line with the center of the pleats. Start 10 cm (4 in) above the lower edge and stitch on rings spaced at 20 cm (8 in) intervals, ending at least 10 cm (4 in) below the base of the pleat stitching (diagram 4).

DIAGRAM **4**

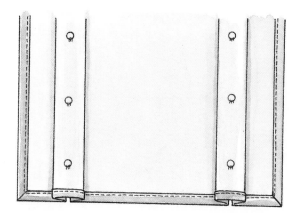

7   Cut the dowel or lath to match the length between the center of the pleats at the top. Cut a fabric strip 7 cm (2$^3/_4$ in) wide to the same length plus 3 cm (1$^1/_4$ in). Fold the fabric strip in half lengthways with right sides together and raw edges level. Stitch across one short end and the long edge 1 cm ($^3/_8$ in) in from raw edges to make a casing (diagram 5).

DIAGRAM **5**

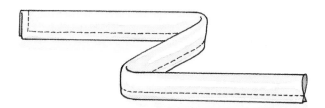

8   Turn the strip right side out and press. Insert the dowel or lath into the casing. Tuck the raw ends of the fabric to the inside and slipstitch them together neatly.

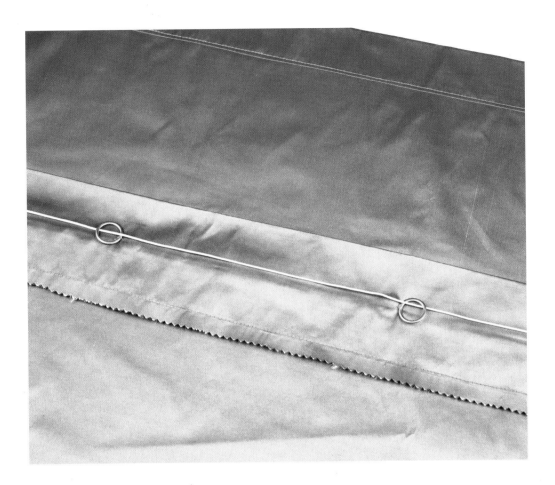

9   Place the casing to the wrong side of the blind just below the lower rings and handstitch each end of the casing to the blind (diagram 6).

10   Stitch tassels to the lower edge of the blind hem in line with the rings at the center of the pleats. Thread the cord and hang the blind in the same way as for the Roman blind, steps 8–10, page 148.

> **NOTE**
> If you need to join the fabric to make up the width required, place the seams at the back folds of the pleats.

DIAGRAM 6

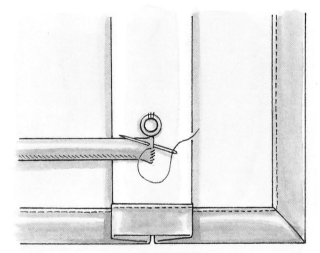

Fabric glossary

Batiste
Fine, sheer, plain woven fabric, usually cotton, used for lightweight curtains.

Broderie anglaise
A decorative embroidered cotton fabric with punched embroidered holes available as both a fabric and edging trim. Available in white and pastel colors and used as a trim on towels, pillowcases and tablecloths.

Calico
A cheap, plain cotton fabric available in various weights and usually in an unbleached cream color. It creases easily and may shrink when washed. Used for inner cushion and pillow covers and trial items.

Cambric
A fine, firm, closely woven plain-weave cotton fabric. Used for inner covers on cushions, pillows and duvets.

Chambray
A fine, woven, cotton fabric with white weft threads and a single color for the warp threads (often blue). The effect is of a fine denim. Used for cushions, curtains and tablecloths.

Chenille
A soft fabric with a thick, velvety pile. Originally made from wool or cotton, it can now also be synthetic. Used for throws, bedcovers and curtains.

Chintz
Medium-weight woven cotton fabric, often printed with a bold floral design, with shiny glazed finish. Used for cushions, curtains, tablecloths and chair covers.

Corduroy
A hard wearing pile fabric with distinctive lengthways cords of pile, available in different weights, from lightweight needlecord to heavyweight elephant cord. Used for cushions.

Crushed velvet
A velvet pile fabric, processed to flatten the pile so the tufts lay in different directions to give an interesting texture. Used for cushions, curtains and bedcovers.

Damask
A firmly woven, self-patterned fabric made on a jacquard loom usually from cotton or a combination of fibers. Traditionally used for tablecloths and napkins.

Denim
Very hardwearing twill-weave, cotton fabric traditionally with white weft threads and blue warp threads, which give a mottled, faded look. Used for cushions, curtains and chair seat covers.

Domett
A very soft, open-weave fabric with a napped surface. Made from cotton or synthetic fibers, domett is used as an interlining between the fabric and the lining in curtains, to add warmth and very light padding.

Drill
A hardwearing, twill-weave, cotton fabric usually plain dyed. Made in various weights. Used for cushions and chair covers.

Flannel
A soft, plain or twill-weave fabric with a flat napped surface usually made from wool. Used for throws, bedcovers and cushions.

Georgette
A fine fabric with a crêpe texture which drapes well and is used for sheer curtains and bed drapes.

Gingham
Lightweight, cotton fabric with white and a single colored yarn woven to form a characteristic check pattern. Available in checks of varying size. Used for lightweight curtains and tablecloths.

Hopsack
A coarse-weave, medium-weight fabric made using two yarns in each direction. Can be made from wool, cotton or synthetic fibres. Used for throws and bedcovers.

Lawn
A lightweight, plain weave, soft cotton fabric used for sheer curtains and bed drapes.

Linen
A very strong fabric with a high luster, made from fibers from the flax plant. Linen fabrics are available in all weights from fine lawn to heavy furnishing fabrics. Most linens crease easily. Used for all types of soft furnishing from window drapes to chair covers.

Lining
A secondary fabric used to back curtains or other fabric items, to improve drape and cut out light, or provide a neat backing. A firmly woven cotton sateen is the most usual and it comes in cream, beige, white and a range of colors.

Matelassé
A thick double cloth with a quilted effect; it is woven from a double set of warp and weft threads which interlink at intervals producing the quilted effect. Used for cushions, throws and bedcovers.

Organdy
A very sheer, cotton fabric with a crisp finish which washing may remove. It

creases very easily. Used for edgings and specialty cushion covers.

Organza

A very sheer, fine fabric similar to organdy but made from silk, viscose or polyester fibers. It creases very easily. Used for edgings and specialty cushion covers.

Piqué

A crisp, light- to medium-weight cotton fabric, often plain white, with a textured surface of fine ribs or a small geometric pattern. Used for tablecloths, napkins, cushions and curtains.

Polycotton

A fabric, usually plain weave, made from a mix of polyester and cotton fibers. This combines the comfort and absorbency of cotton with the crease-resistance and strength of polyester. Used for sheets, duvet covers and pillowcases.

Polyester

A versatile synthetic fiber, polyester can be spun to imitate the natural fibers – cotton, wool, silk and linen. It is strong and crease-resistant and is often mixed with natural fibers to add these qualities.

Poplin

A medium-weight, hardwearing, plain weave fabric with a slight surface sheen. It is usually made from cotton, or a mixture of polyester and cotton fibers. Used for sheeting, pillowcases and duvet covers.

Sateen

A strong, plain cotton fabric woven to give a shiny smooth surface on the right side and a matt finish on the wrong side. It is mainly used for lining curtains.

Sheeting

An extra wide fabric, usually a polyester/cotton mixture, produced especially wide enough to make sheets and duvet covers.

Silk

Soft but strong, silk fibers are obtained from the cocoons of silk worms. Silk fibers absorb dyes easily to produce a good range of deep colors and can be woven into various fabrics. Used for cushion covers, table runners and curtains.

Silk dupion

A medium-weight fabric with a fine but uneven slub weave caused by the natural thickening of the silk fibers in some areas. Used for cushion covers, table runners and curtains.

Toile de jouy

A traditional cotton print in a single color on a beige or off-white background. The prints typically show romantic rustic scenes of figures and foliage. Used for curtains, cushions, tablecloths and chair covers.

Twill

A type of weave which forms diagonal lines on the right side of the fabric. There are various types of twill weaves and any fibers can be woven this way.

Velvet

A woven fabric with a surface pile. Originally made from silk, now it is often made from cotton or polyester. Used for cushions, curtains and throws.

Voile

A fine, lightweight, slightly open-weave fabric made from cotton, polyester or a mixture of the two. Used for sheer curtains and bed drapes.

Wool

Made from sheep's fleece, woollen fabrics are hard wearing, hairy and warm, and easy to mold. Wool, like silk, can be made into many different fabrics and weights varying from very fine to heavyweight. Most often used for blankets, throws, bedcovers or cushion covers.

Suppliers and useful addresses

UNITED STATES

Jo-Ann Stores, Inc.
5555 Darrow Road
Hudson, OH 44236
Tel: (330) 656-2600
Email:guest.services@jo-annstores.com
www.joann.com
National retail franchise offering fabrics,
sewing and craft supplies and related
merchandise.

Ben Franklin Crafts
www2.benfranklinstores.com
National franchise of independently
owned craft stores featuring fabrics,
home décor, craft supplies and related
merchandise.

Hancock Fabrics
One Fashion Way
Baldwyn, Mississippi 38824
Tel: (877) 322-7427
www.hancockfabrics.com
National retailer offering fabrics, craft
supplies and related merchandise.

Rag Shop
111 Wagaraw Road
Hawthorne, NJ 07506
Tel: (973) 423-1303
Email: generalinfo@ragshop.com
www.ragshop.com
East Coast retailer offering fabrics, craft
supplies and related merchandise.

Hobby Lobby Stores Inc.
7707 S.W. 44th St.
Oklahoma City, OK 73179
Tel: (405) 745-1100
www.hobbylobby.com
National retailer offering fabrics, crafts,
home accents and related merchandise.

CANADA

Fabricland/Fabricville
www.fabricland.ca/
Canadian retailer with more than
170 stores offering fabrics, sewing
supplies, home décor items and related
merchandise.

ONLINE RETAILERS

Fabric.com
2151 Northwest Parkway, Suite 500
Marietta, GA 30067
Tel: (888) 455-2940
Email: customercare@fabric.com
www.fabric.com
Online retailer offering fabrics, notions,
sewing machines.

Main Street Bedding Company/The
Fabric House
123 East Unaka Ave.
Johnson City, TN 37601
Tel: (423) 929-2260
Email: BeddingCo@aol.com
www.mainstreetbeddingcompany.com
Online retailer offering decorator fabrics
and custom home décor items.

UK

Baer & Ingram
Dragon Works
Leigh on Mendip
Radstock BA3 5QZ
Tel: 01373 813800
Email: sales@baer-ingram.co.uk
www.baer-ingram.co.uk
Wide range of cotton fabrics available
mail order.

Fabric World
287 High Street
Sutton
Surrey SM1 1LL
Tel: 020 8643 5127
Email: info@fabricworldlondon.co.uk
www.fabricworldlondon.co.uk
Fabric stockists, also available mail
order by email.

G P & J Baker
Chelsea Harbour Design Centre
North Dome G18/19
London SW10 0XE
Tel: 020 7351 7760
www.gpjbaker.co.uk
Suppliers of top quality curtain and soft
furnishing fabrics.

John Lewis
Oxford Street
London
W1A 1EX
Tel: 020 7629 7711
www.johnlewis.com
Stocks a range of furnishing fabrics and
accessories. Visit the website for details
of branches nationwide.

MacCulloch & Wallis Limited
25–26 Dering Street
London
W1R 0BH
Tel: 020 7629 0311
Fax: 020 7491 2481
Email: macculloch@psilink.co.uk
www.macculloch-wallis.co.uk
Stockists of a range of fabrics, sewing
equipment and haberdashery supplies.

Malabar
31-33 The South Bank Business Centre
Ponton Road
London
SW8 5BL
Tel: 020 7501 4200
Fax: 020 7501 4210
Email: info@malabar.co.uk
www.malabar.co.uk
Designer and stockist of fabrics
available through selected stockists.

Marvic Textiles Ltd
Chelsea Harbour Design Centre
Chelsea Harbour
London
SW10 0XE
Tel: 020 7352 3119
Large range of fabrics available for soft
furnishing and upholstery.

Index

Acknowledgments

The author and publishers would like to thank the following people for their contributions to this book:

Gwen Diamond, Vicky French, and Melanie Williams for their expert stitching.

Martin Short for sourcing such wonderful fabrics.

Elizabeth Johnson and Sophie Silocchi for letting us photograph in their homes.

Baer & Ingram, GP&J Baker, Lewis & Wood, Malabar, and Marvic for generously donating fabric to make up the projects. For full details, see page 158.